Mithras

Mithras

Mysteries and
Initiation
Rediscovered

D. Jason Cooper

SAMUEL WEISER, INC.

York Beach, Maine

First published in 1996 by
Samuel Weiser, Inc.
P. O. Box 612
York Beach, ME 03910-0612

Library of Congress Cataloging-in-Publication Data

Cooper, D. Jason
   Mithras: mysteries and initiation rediscovered /
D. Jason Cooper.
      p.   cm.
   Includes bibliographical references (p.   ) and
index.
   (pbk.: alk. paper)
   1. Mithraism. I. Title.
BL 1585.C66 1996
299'.15--dc20   96-10326
                                                CIP

ISBN 0-87728-865-8
MG

Cover art is Mithras, The Prophet, the right-hand panel of the arch of the
Dura Mithraeum of Dura-Europos, Syria, reconstruction at Yale University
Art Gallery. From the Dura-Europos Collection (Yale 78),
photograph copyright © Yale University Art Gallery.
Used by permission.

Typeset in 11 point Windsor Light

Printed in the United States of America

04 03 01 00 99 98 97 96
10 9 8 7 6 5 4 3 2 1

*The paper used in this publication meets the minimum requirements of the
American National Standard for Permanence of Paper for Printed Library
Materials Z39.48-1984.*

To Three Servants of the Hermetic Kings,
Citizens of the Empire of Wisdom:
Alistair, Ray, and 'Tino

TABLE OF CONTENTS

INTRODUCTION

His worship has lasted over 3,500 years and continues to this day. For almost 500 years his religion vied with Christianity for dominance of Rome and through that the whole of Western Civilization. In ancient times he found followers in the Indian, Persian, and Roman Empires, and as far north as the Russian steppes. Today Mithras counts followers in India, Iran, the United States, Canada, the United Kingdom, Australia, New Zealand and elsewhere. Known as Mitra to the Indians, Mithra to the Iranis and Zarathustrians and Mithras to the Romans, this god is the oldest of all living deities.

Mithras has been worshipped in more religious traditions than perhaps any other deity in history. Aryan tribal pagans, Hindus, Iranian pagans, Zarathustrians, the Mitanni people of the Middle East, the Romans, and even the Manicheans have all worshipped him. In the Roman Empire, his followers formed one of the mystery religions. Each of the seven degrees of initiation had its own esoteric, moral, and ritual principles which led the follower deeper into the secrets of the god.

Roman Mithrasism taught concepts of esoteric anatomy and adeptship. It may even have had a secret form of astrology with an alternative system of signs and portents.

But for all this, occultists have largely ignored Mithras. Few know anything about him, and fewer still have written more than the odd line about him.

Yet no book written by an occultist or directed to occultists has treated this ancient tradition. This book is designed to redress that imbalance by examining Mithras and the religion which bears his name—a religion which very nearly became the foundation of our modern world.

Mithras: Mysteries and Initiation Rediscovered concentrates on the Roman mystery religion of Mithrasism, whose god contended with Christ on equal terms for almost five hundred years.[1] In fact, contemporary writers recognized Mithrasism as the greatest rival to early Christianity—a greater threat even than the religion of Isis. Indeed, in retrospect there is every reason to believe that if Rome had not become Christian, it would have become Mithrasian.

To combat the threat, Christian writers went to extraordinary lengths and indulged in extremely underhanded tactics. They claimed Mithrasians had stolen Christian theology and ritual, although clearly the Mithrasian religion embraced that theology and those rituals earlier than Christianity's existence. Then Christian writers changed the story, saying the Devil, knowing in advance of the coming of the Christian sacraments, imitated them before they existed in order to denigrate them.

Mithrasism did have a sacrament which strongly resembled a Christian rite. It included wine as a symbol of sacrificial blood and used bread in wafers or small loaves marked with a cross to symbolize flesh. And other parallels abound. Mithrasians called themselves "brother" and were led by a priest called a "father" whose symbols were his staff and ring, his hat, and a hooked sword. Christianity adopted the hook and staff as the shepherd's crook; the hat became stiffened and was called a Miter (the name came from the name of the god, Mithras); the ring remained. Thus was derived the symbolic heraldry of the bishop. Similarly, Mithrasian priests were ruled by a "father of fathers" who lived in Rome. This "father of fathers," like the Pope, was elected by a council of priests. The religion of Mithras, though, set the number of that council at ten. In many other ways the Mithrasians predated the Christians in precisely those areas which are supposedly identifiably and uniquely Christian.

But there were many differences, too. Mithras appealed to a different kind of follower than Christ. He offered a salvation based, not only on faith and compassion, but also on knowledge and val-

---

[1] The common practice, set by Cumont, is to drop the *s* from the root word Mithras before forming its variants (e.g., Mithraist, Mithraic, etc.). This spelling emphasizes the continuity between the Iranian and Roman deities. In order to differentiate between the two, however, I prefer in this work to retain the *s* (e.g., Mithrasist, Mithrasic, etc.).

or. In this he appealed not only to the poor, the slave and the freed-man, but to the traditionalist Roman aristocracy, soldiers, and honest merchants as well. Even some Emperors followed him. Mithras posed no threat to the traditions and civilization of Rome. The new god made peace with the old gods, Jupiter, Saturn, Ocean-us, Venus, and Sol. He made peace, too, with the newer gods, Isis and Serapis.

Christ made no such accommodation. When the Christians gained ascendancy, they took the churches of Isis and made them their own. They destroyed all the liturgies of other gods. And they attacked Mithras. They attacked his temples with axes. They smashed the sacred statuary. They burned his books and attacked his followers. They dumped rubbish and the refuse of graveyards in his temples to desecrate them, and built their own churches on the ruins of Mithrasian temples. In one case they murdered his priest and left the corpse on the altar. They sought in every way to wipe the memory of the god Mithras from the face of the earth.

But in the end, they failed. The temples remained and over the past century, have been yielding up their secrets to scholars engaged in the painstaking task of reconstructing Mithrasism. Moreover, the recovery process is revealing a final secret of Mithras, a secret long beyond the reach of any mortal—Christian or otherwise. Hid-den in the god's secret name (Meitras), in the icon through which he was most worshipped, and in the degrees of initiation he taught, this secret has endured, as invincible as the god's title "invictus" promised. Despite attempts to destroy it, Mithra's final secret has remained untouched, pure, and open to those who seek it.

Mithras

Chapter 1

The Nature of Mithras

When the Aryan tribes swept down from the Russian steppes they brought their gods with them. Some time between 2000 and 1500 B.C.E., these tribes entered India and Iran, bringing with them one particular deity whom they called respectively Mitra, or Mithra.

A horse-born branch of the Aryan tribe which conquered a Middle Eastern kingdom, actually named their new empire after the deity. These people, the Mitanni, gave us the first written reference to Mitra in a treaty between themselves and the Hittites. Signed about 1375 B.C.E., the treaty calls on divine witnesses to pledge its terms. The Hittites called on the sun god. The Mitanni called on Mitra.

Mitra had been worshipped by the Iranians for centuries when Zarathustra (we call him Zoroaster, the Greek version of his name) founded the first revealed religion. Zarathustra announced the primacy of Ahura Mazda, the Wise Lord, who was served by the Amentas Spenta, or bounteous immortals. Among these was Mithra, whom Ahura Mazda declared to be "as worthy of worship as myself."[1] Thus the Zarathustrian reform did not replace Mithra in the Iranian Pantheon. It merely changed his role.

Mithra may also have been worshipped by the Mani. Some branches of Manicheism identified Mithra as the ruler of the second or third emanation (an occultist would say "ray," "aeon," or "sepheroth"). But whether there were actual rites of worship ded-

---

[1] Ilya Gershevitch, *The Avestan Hymn to Mithra* (Cambridge, England: Cambridge University Press, 1959) p. 75. The announcement is in fact made at the opening of the Yasht, in the first verse.

icated to him or whether he simply functioned as an anthropomorphic principle is impossible to say.

In the Roman Empire, this same deity was called Mithras, and was the central figure of a mystery religion that for almost five hundred years vied with Christianity for dominance. Roman Mithrasism differed so markedly, however, from other traditions that some scholars have claimed Mithras to be a unique deity, distinct from Mitra or Mithra. Although this book deals primarily with Mithrasism in its Roman form, it will demonstrate that there is good reason to connect the Roman Mithras with his other forms in other traditions.

In the Beginning was a Word

The names Mitra, Mithra, and Mithras all derive from the Indo-European root "Mihr," which translates both as "friend" and as "contract." While both translations are correct however, neither gives a full account of the word. "Mihr" itself derives from "mei," an Indo-European root meaning "exchange." But Aryan society did not use the word "exchange" to describe a transaction.

Ancient societies were hierarchical. Neither the concept of an exchange between equals after which a relationship ended (our meaning of contract), nor the concept of an open-ended exchange between equals (our meaning of friendship) were contained in the original meaning of the words "mihr" or "mei." (For our concept of friendship, the Ṛg Veda uses the word "sakhi.") The friendship or contract offered by Mihr, or Mitra as he became known, was an exchange between unequal partners with Mitra as a just lord. Like any feudal relationship, this "friendship" imposed certain obligations on both sides. Mitra oversaw the affairs of his worshippers. He established justice for them. In return, his worshippers had to be upright in their dealings with others. Mitra was thus "lord of the contract" (a title frequently applied to him), more powerful and knowledgeable than his worshippers (a valuable attribute for a god). He stood between parties as a judge, upholding the sacredness of the exchange, the "mei."

This concept of a "god of the exchange" naturally led to a doctrine of reciprocal responsibility: those who follow his rule the god protects; those who defy it by deceitful or dishonest action he punishes. For a god to be effective in this role, he had to have the power to know what was right and enforce it. Moreover there had to be a means of making the will of the god known. This was done by the ordeal of fire.

In a dispute over a contract, a man could choose to run through a narrow strip of earth with bonfires on either side. If he lived, he was said to have been spared by Mitra and was considered innocent. In later eras, molten copper was poured over his breast. If he lived, he was declared to have passed the test. Impossible as it sounds to us, there were occasions when people did choose to go through the agony, and emerged vindicated. But the god of the Aryans had other aspects, too.

A god who enforces the contract must know what really happens between men talking in private. To see things from a distance in a primitive society, gaining such a vantage point was seen as a function of distance. A person on a mountain sees more than one in a valley. A god in the sky sees more than a person on a mountain. Thus, Mitra, already a god of fire, became a god of the stars and sun. The stars became his eyes, so he came to be called the god of ten thousand eyes. His hearing was similarly exalted. Whether his followers prayed in a shout or a whisper, Mitra heard. He also became associated with cattle and was portrayed as the ruler or giver of broad pastures. As time went on, other attributes came to be associated with Mitra as he appeared in different traditions in different places.

The Indian Mitra

Our primary source of information on the Indian god Mitra is the Ṛg Veda which, although written down about 1500 B.C.E., may have been composed some three hundred years earlier. Mitra was originally an important deity to the Indians. But since the reformation and the primacy of Brahma, Vishnu, and Siva, he has ceased to be actively worshipped in the Hindu tradition.

In Vedic references, Mitra is normally mentioned with a partner, Varuna. In fact there are only a dozen references to either god alone, but over a hundred of the two together. I believe that, like the Nasati, Mitra and Varuna may originally have been twins. This would explain why the two gods are so similar, why they are mentioned together, and why they are linked to paired principles. Mitra is identified with fire, earth, the color red, morning and day, and the right-hand side; Varuna with water, heaven, evening and night, and the left-hand side. Just as Mitra had the ordeal by fire, so Varuna had the ordeal by water. When a man was accused of breaking an oath he would immerse himself under water by holding another man's legs. An arrow was shot as he went under and a swift man was sent to fetch the arrow where it landed. If the runner returned before the man drowned, Varuna had spared him.

The sort of duality Mitra-Varuna displays is an important part of Vedic thought. Between them, the two gods encompass the universe and rule it in the same way they rule the affairs of men. That is, just as they bring order to the world of men, so they bring order to the functions of the universe. To break the law of the god, then, is akin to breaking a natural law. Like his Aryan tribal counterpart, Mitra is a god who sees both righteousness and transgression and gives benefit or retribution accordingly.

Thus Mitra's eye is the sun and he sets it on its course. For this reason prayers are addressed to him at sunrise and his blessing is asked for the coming day. Moreover, while Mitra often punishes transgressors with sickness, particularly leprosy, he is not a terrible god. In fact, Mitra is the first god credited with recognizing and rewarding true penance. He will punish sin but, for those who truly repent, he will also forgive it.

Other features of the tribal god were retained by Mitra in the Vedic tradition, for instance his association with cattle.[2] Cattle

---

[2] Mithras' complex relationship with Varuna is shown well here. For example, single cattle (ones tied with rope) refer to Varuna. Domesticated herds refer to Mitra, reinforcing Iranian Mithra's title as "lord of the wide pastures."

were sacrificed to him. On his worshippers he bestowed gifts, including wide pastures, large herds, male children, and beautiful women. And like Mithra and Mithras, Mitra was a chariot-driving god. Mitra was also associated with a plant named Soma whose juices, often mixed with cows' milk, produced intoxication. The plant was called the "averter of death," and was used to stimulate astral travel to allow the priests of Mitra to see beyond the veil of death. In the act of producing the drink, the plant was described as being "sacrificed."

There is a myth attached to the crushing of the Soma plant. In it the gods conspire to kill their fellow deity Soma. Mitra refuses, saying his name means "friend." He is told the other gods will kill Soma anyway, but that without the milk from Mitra's cattle to produce the magic drink, benefit of this death will not be widely distributed. Reluctantly, Mitra takes part in the plot. Soma is killed and, through his death, others become immortal. But Mitra's cattle are upset with his part in the plot and confront the god. He explains to them the murder was not his doing.

This myth is sometimes identified as the origin of the bull-slaying central to the worship of the Roman Mithras. It depends on an astrological association of both plants and cattle to the Moon. While this is possible, the slaying of the bull may have come from any one of a number of sources—if indeed it can be said to have only one source.

The Iranian Mithra and Zarathustra

As the Aryan tribes swept south, they split into two major branches, the Indians in the east and the Iranis in the west. Both worshipped the god of the contract in similar ways. Like the Indians, the Iranis sacrificed cattle to Mithra. They invoked him to preserve the sanctity of the contract. They associated him with fire. And like both Indian and Roman worshippers, the Iranis concluded contracts before fires so that they might be made in the presence of Mithra. Like Mitra, Mithra saw all things. The Avestan Yast (hymn) dedicated to him describes him as having a thousand ears, ten thousand eyes, and as never sleeping.[3] And like Mitra, Mithra has a partner, Apam Nepat, whose name means Grandson of Waters. (Note that the same elemental connection of fire and water is maintained as in the Indian tradition.)

Mithra was a moral god, upholding the sanctity of the contract even when that contract was made with one who was sure to break it. His primary responsibility was to the rightness of the action. In this he stood above the various national gods of the time, who had little function other than to look after the welfare of the state and its wealthiest members. In fact, Mithra was the first such moral deity, and stands above the notions of many worshippers of many gods today.

Mithra was judge not only the contracts between individuals but the pledges given between nations. He set boundaries between neighbors and nations alike, for he was still the lord of the wide pastures. In this he was a supranational god—a god who for the first time in history put the value of truth above the interests of his own cult, his own followers, his own nation.

Like Mitra, Mithra was still the god who saw and heard all, having a thousand ears, a thousand eyes, and ten thousand spies. But the Iranian Mithra is a warrior god while Mitra of India was not. Countries who broke their word faced the wrath of Mithra. Mithra is frequently called "the one who calls people to account" and his punishments are both detailed and specific.

Why should Mithra be more warlike than Mitra? Possibly because the Iranis had no equivalent to the Indians' Indra. Without a specific god of national conquest some of Indra's warlike nature was transferred to Mithra. But where Indra was simply a god of national conquest, Mithra had that additional and essential dimension of morality.

---

[3] Gershevitch, *Avestan Hymn to Mithra*, p. 77. This, verse 7, is the first instance of this description. There are several more which repeat the wording exactly.

Mithra punishes the impious. Frequently this is by diseases such as leprosy. But he has more physical punishments. His chariot of war in which he sets out to fight evil is drawn by four horses. He has two companions with him in this fight: Sraosha (obedience to the law or feudal obligations) and Rashnu (Truest, the lord of the ordeal). With him, too, is Verethraghna, or Victory, who can take the form of a boar, the wind, or a golden-horned bull. In this chariot Mithra conquers the armies of evil. The description of the chariot lists the various axes, spears, and other weapons that it carried, making it a fearsome token of Mithra's invincible power.

The Iranis had a deep reverence for Mithra, as is proved by their reception of the prophet, Zarathustra. Zarathustra is the most important person in the recorded history of religion, bar none. The first man to promulgate a divinely revealed religion, he influenced the religions of Judaism, Christianity, Mithrasism, Islam, northern (Mahayana) Buddhism, Manicheism, and the pagan Norse myths. Over half the world has accepted a significant portion of his precepts under the guise of one or another of these faiths.

At the age of about forty Zarathustra, a priest in the traditional Irani rites, received a revelation. In it, the many gods of the Iranis were supplanted by a new deity who was the supreme deity of the Good. This deity became known as Ahura Mazda, or the "Wise Lord." Opposed to Ahura Mazda was Aingra Mainyu or Ahriman, the "Angry Spirit," the chief deity of evil. Both deities had underlings and partners. The chief allies of Ahura Mazda were the "Amentas Spenta." Created by the "Wise Lord ," these "Bounteous" or "Holy Immortals" included Mithra.

There is a hymn to Mithra in the Zarathustrian holy work, the *Avesta*. It is a beautiful hymn, or Yast, and Ilya Gershevitch is right to lament that it is not more widely known.[4] In it, Ahura Mazda addresses the prophet Zarathustra, saying that when he created

[4] Gershevitch, *Avestan Hymn to Mithra*, p. vii.

Mithra, he made him as worthy of worship as himself. This accolade is given to no other Amenta Spenta or Yazata. Historians have argued that this distinction indicates only that the cult of Mithra was so important that Zarathustra had to give its god special concessions to convert its members. Some have even argued the popularity from the concessions. But there is another theological reason for the special attention given to Mithra by Zarathustra.

Mitra-Varuna was a fire-water duality. Mithra-Apam Nepat, was also a fire-water duality which predated the revelation of Zarathustra. The symbol Zarathustra chose for the good, and for the natural order of things he conceived good to be, was purifying fire. This took both a physical and a spiritual form.

So it was natural that the god of the fire ordeal, who set the affairs of men and the natural universe in order, should be considered supreme among Ahura Mazda's creations.

Mithra is a pacifier of lands in turmoil and a supporter of government regularity. He supports authority but opposes governments which are vexatious of the people. In this he is a judge of kings, supporting those who keep their word and reign justly, while overthrowing those who do not.

Like Mitra, Mithra was associated with the ritual consumption of a plant, the Haoma, which recalls the Indian Soma. Again, the Haoma plant was crushed and its juices drunk as a ritual reminder of a time of immortality in a primeval religious past. Worshippers hoped to take part in that immortality again, as Zarathustra promised. This sacrament of the bread and wine made flesh and blood, Zarathustra established as early as 650 B.C.E., and the Mithrasians continued the practice.

Mithra is a much more fully developed image than the rather ethereal Mitra. Unlike the Indian god, we actually have a relief of the Iranian deity. Reconstruction shows Mithra shaking hands with King Antiochus. It is Mithra's attire, however, that is important to the current study. Mithra wears the Phrygian cap, Persian trousers, and a cape. His hat is star speckled (from textual evidence his chariot is similarly decorated). Rays of light emerge from Mithra's head much like a halo. His choke collar is a serpent. This image, or one very like it, will appear again in Rome.

Mithras, the Roman Mystery God

There is great controversy over the connection between the Roman Mithras and the Iranian Mithra. In fact, some scholars like David Ulansey[5] and Michael P. Speidel[6] have argued that they are distinct deities. Ulansey maintains that Mithras is a reformed Perseus, while Speidel claims that he is a reformed Orion.

Part of the problem is what we have to work with. For the Indian Mitra and the Iranian Mithra, we rely almost exclusively on textual evidence. For the Indian Mitra we have the Ŗg Veda. For Mithra we have the Yasts (hymns) of the Zarathustrian holy work, *The Avesta*, and the inscriptions of kings such as Darius the Great. For the god of the Aryan tribes, we have only anthropological evidence or reconstructions from lingual drift.

For the Roman Mithras, however, we have almost no textual evidence except some inscriptions dedicating sacrifices, some graffiti on temple walls, and some explanatory notes in murals which have survived. There is also some contemporary polemic from Christian writers (like Tertullian) or the comments of pagan observers (like Porphory).

Apart from that, however, what we know of Mithras must be gained from archeology. Excavations of his temples have given us murals, statues, mosaics, altars, and even the floor plans of the temples. But no book remains. The problem has been likened to trying to understand Christianity with nothing more than the Old Testament and the Medieval cathedrals from which to work.

The founder of Mithrasian studies, Franz Cumont, believed in a very close relationship between the Roman and the Iranian religions. So close, in fact, that he argued the Iranians carried out certain rites because the Roman Mithrasians performed them. Such was his authority in the field that his view was not questioned for over forty years.

[5] David Ulansey, *The Origins of the Mithraic Mysteries: Cosmology and Salvation in the Ancient World* (London and New York: Oxford University Press, 1990), pp. 25-27 provide the core of the identification.
[6] Michael P. Speidel, *Mithras-Orion: Greek Hero and Roman Army God* (Leiden: E.J. Brill, 1980), p. i.

More recently, a number of scholars have raised doubts about this relationship. How, for example, could the two religions have cooperated? After all, the Roman and Persian Empires were deadly enemies. It would seem unlikely that their priests would get together to work out a consistent theology.

Once Cumont's theory came under question a wide variety of alternative theories were suggested, for instance, those of Ulansey and Speidel mentioned above. It has been suggested we've found no literature of Mithras simply because there wasn't any: the religion contained no secrets, no theology, and was in effect little more than an excuse for drunken revelry.[7] The long-accepted Mithras-Christ rivalry has also been cast into doubt. It has been suggested the mystery religion was no more than a backwater of pagan thought. It has even been suggested Christianity came first and the followers of Mithras imitated Christianity, though history proved that untrue 2000 years ago.

We'll examine these notions in the coming chapters, looking at them in a different light, and seeing the Mithrasians as they would have seen themselves: as members of a mystery religion, as followers of a god who gave secrets in return for loyalty and wisdom in discrete stages if certain tests were passed. Once we look with occult eyes, the story of Mithrasism becomes much clearer.

The God

Mithras is portrayed as a young man, certainly no older than his early thirties. He wears Persian trousers, a Phrygian cap with its characteristic forward folding top, and a cloak which normally billows out behind him to reveal an underside which is frequently speckled with eight-pointed stars. The cloak is attached by a broach on his right shoulder. Mithras' characteristic pose is holding down a bull. One hand holds the bull's horn or muzzle, a knee is in the

---

[7] Walter Burkert, *Ancient Mystery Cults* (Cambridge: Harvard University Press, 1987). See, for example, page 110 which puts the wine bowl and full meals at the center of Mithrasian worship.

bull's back. With his other hand, Mithras is about to, or has already, plunged a dagger into the bull's shoulder.

This act of sacrificing the bull is central to the entire religion of Mithrasism. The bull-slaying scene appears in every temple of the god throughout the entire Roman Empire. Mithras is usually portrayed with two companions, miniature versions of himself, called Cautes and Cautopates. These are his torchbearers, one holding the torch aloft and the other pointing it down. The theology and inner meaning of these symbols will become apparent as this study progresses. For now, let us examine the connection between Mithras and Mithra.

The Transfer

Two Roman historians, Plutarch of the first century CE and Appian[8] of the second, recount learn how Mithras was brought to the West.

The soldiers of Mithridates Eupator taught the initiation secrets of Mithra to the Cilician pirates. When Pompey defeated these pirates in 67 B.C.E., he settled them in Greece. In doing this the mysteries of Mithras were brought to the West.[9]

If we accept these two accounts, much of the theology of Mithrasism becomes clear. And in the light of the fact there is no logical reason to dispute the story, the word of witnesses closer to the events should generally be accepted. For instance, they solve the problem of how Roman and Persian priests could work out a consistent theology by showing that the two religions in fact had a common origin. Moreover, the Cilicians, being seamen, probably engaged in the trade between the Roman and Persian Empires

---

[8] M. J. Vermaseren, *Mithras: The Secret God* (London: Chatto & Windus, 1959), p. 27 gives the story of both historians as one.
[9] Per Beskow, "The Routes of Early Mithrasism," in Actes de Congrès, *Etudes Mithriaques* (Bibliothèque Pahlavi, Tehran-Liège, 1978), pp. 12-13. Some scholars, like Beskow, have lately called this theory into serious question. But there is nothing improbable or unlikely in Plutarch's and Appian's accounts, though they may lack physical proof of the sort archeology cannot provide.

which went on unabated despite the wars between them. This trade doubtless took the Cilicians to Persian ports, where they found Zarathustrian temples in which priests, or Magi, taught Mithrasian theology and rituals from books now lost to us. The Cilicians would then have disseminated these teachings along trade routes.

The theology these merchants found in Persian ports would not have been a formal doctrine. Religion had not yet been reduced from a divine vision to a prototypal party platform. What might now be considered schismatic was tolerated among Mithrasians. In fact, some theological variation did creep into Roman Mithrasism. There were clearly regions—the Danube, Syria, Rome—where different opinions held sway.

But why would a group of expatriate pirates have a complex and theologically sophisticated religion? A little background may help to explain. Cilicia was a province on the south central coast of Asia Minor, in what is now Turkey. It boasted two major cities, Tarsus (as in Paul of...) and Tyana (as in the pagan prophet Apollonius). The pirates of Pompey's adventure, Plutarch tells us, had over a thousand ships and captured over four hundred cities. There were about twenty thousand of them in all. These were not pirates in our sense of the word, however, but privateers fighting a war in which robbery became a tactic. They fought Rome on sea while their ally, Mithridates (meaning "gift of Mithra") fought them on land. The two groups were allies. Both gained their greatest strength during the Roman Social Wars which brought down the Republic.

Plutarch[10] tells us that, as the pirates gained strength, they were joined by men of ability, men of noble rank, and men of wealth, forming in fact a maritime nation in embryo. They provided a useful foil for Mithridates, who conquered much of Asia Minor and ruled it for twenty years until finally defeated by Pompey.

When Pompey did succeed in both the land and sea campaigns, he settled the pirates in Greece, along with all their cultural and

---

[10] Plutarch, *Fall of the Roman Republic: Six Lives by Plutarch*, trans. Rex Warner (London: Penguin, 1958), p. 160. Mithras is also mentioned here.

theological baggage. As the Cilicians settled into their new life, their religion began to gather adherents. But the new members were not drawn randomly from Roman society. Some groups were more attracted to the new religion than others. Indeed, the same sort of men who originally became pirates tended to espouse Mithrasism: men of military rank, men of nobility, and men of wealth. In general, they were devoutly honest and of high character, a fact vouched for by Pompey's trust in them and his decision to relocate them in Greece. For these "pirates," had they won, would have been called freedom fighters.

Chapter 2

The Nature of the Cult

Most people acknowledge the period from Augustus to the fall of Rome as fundamental to our own history. During this time, the religious foundations of almost two thousand years of cultural history were laid. But those foundations were not secure: Christianity's triumph then was no more assured than its survival today. To thoroughly understand those times, we need to examine those foundations more closely and to ask, "Could the West have become a Mithrasic world?"

For a long time it was accepted Rome was simply tired of its adopted Greek pantheon. There were too many gods for an Empire held together only by efficient administration and an army. It seemed clear to all that some Emperor would eventually impose a monotheistic religion upon Rome, paralleling in theology the position of the Emperor himself.

There were only three real contenders for the honor of Imperial religion: Christianity, the cult of Sol Invictus, and Mithrasism. It was the Emperor Constantine who eventually made the choice. Though only baptized a Christian on his deathbed, Constantines's administrative policies helped open the doors to establish Christianity as an accepted sect, then as a dominant cult, and finally as the only religion accepted throughout the Empire.

Or so historians long believed. But there is a great deal wrong with this picture. It ignores one of the largest potentially unifying religions, one more highly organized than Christianity: the religion of Isis. It also ignores the depth of theology and loyalty in cults such as that of Dionysus Zagreus or the Gnostics. In fact, many

religions might have formed the theological and sacerdotal counterpart of the power of the Emperor—not the least of which was
the cult of the Emperor itself.

I.A. Richmond suggests the appeal of Mithrasism was too
narrow to ever be a mass movement sufficient to threaten Christianity or unify the Empire. He points to the small size of the temples of Mithras. These were never built to hold more than a few
dozen people; most held only a dozen or so.

I think historians have indulged too much in the notion than
events cast their shadow before their arrival. They have assumed
Christianity's triumph means any difference between Christianity
and another religion must be to the detriment of the other religion.

Had the religions of Mithras, Isis, Dionysus Zagreus or—come
to that—Buddhism (which was also preached in Rome at this time)
triumphed, then they would have shaped society differently. We
cannot look at those religions from our world of centuries of Christian domination and expect from that perspective to explain why
Christianity triumphed and Mithras did not. To do so is to put the
cart before the horse.

If we do not have to accept Renan's dictum, "If the growth of
Christianity had been halted by some mortal illness, the world
would have become Mithraic,"[1] nor do we have to accept Christianity's triumph as pre-ordained. In this context we will take a detailed
look at the organization of the followers of the god.

The Followers

The majority of Mithrasians seem to have been soldiers, often of
high rank, if we are to judge from the inscriptions of votive offerings. The high ranks shouldn't surprise us. People of higher position are the ones who have the money to make offerings to a god.

But Mithras was not only a soldier's god. Inscriptions from the
London temple to Mithras show a high proportion of merchant

[1] Quoted in Walter Burkert, *Ancient Mystery Cults* (Cambridge, MA: Harvard University Press, 1987) p. 3.

followers, at least one merchant was a legion veteran. The names of merchants, usually with eastern names (possibly Syrians) are also recorded in Mithrasic temples at Rome.

Imperial bureaucrats also joined. In Poetovio there were high ranking customs officials. In other areas provincial legates and governors were members.

Roman nobility also joined. Emperors Trajan and Commodus were initiated into the religion. A number of noble houses dedicated a room to the worship of Mithras. For example, one home on the Aventine hill—a luxury quarter then as now—was owned by those who came to Rome with the Severan Emperors. The site is now covered by the Basilica of St. Prisca, but for some time it housed a temple to Mithras.

These groups, particularly the first three, dominated the higher ranks of Mithrasism. But a number of inscriptions were presented to the god from slaves and freedmen (ex-slaves). Such inscriptions are relatively few, but their existence is important in helping establish the nature of the movement.

One of the most intriguing elements of the Mithrasian religion is that it seems to have excluded women. There are a few inscriptions in which women's names appear, but they are never given the title of an official post or a degree of initiation. The surviving murals do not show women at all, only men.

There is one tantalizing exception, however. A grave in Guigariche contains a husband and wife. He is called a lion, she a lioness. There is nothing else to show they were members of the Mithrasian religion. No other symbols of the religion are shown and no mention is made of the god. Nor do we know of any Mithrasian community in the town—then or at any other time.

It seems to offer so much, and yet mean so little, for there are so many other explanations. The terms could simply have been endearments, nicknames for each other which relatives recorded on their graves. The animals could simply have been a totem of the family, referring perhaps to the lion symbol of the Etruscans. Since the graves are in the north of Italy it is possible that this constituted a last defiant stand by what had become a backward and persecuted minority. Or the animals could simply have been a reference to nobility of spirit. They are used as such in Aesop's fables, without any initiatory intent.

Indeed, though we may know the degrees of the Mithrasian religion, there is no indication that they were generally known then. There is, however, a brief, tantalizing reference in Porphyry's *De Abstinentia*[2] to those initiated in the mysteries of Mithras being called lions (if men), or hyenas (if women). The text is corrupt, and "hyania" may originally have been "leaina" or lioness. It may equally have been something else altogether. And this reference may have no bearing on the grave at Guligariche. We cannot stretch the meager evidence far enough to deduce any significant role for women in the religion. In fact, they seem to have been generally excluded.

This may seem strange to modern eyes, but it was commonplace at the time. Various deities accepted only men (the cult of *Bona Dea*) or only women (the cult of Cybele and Attis). Others allowed women only a subsidiary or submissive role (Judaism and Christianity).

Moreover, the religion of Mithras developed certain arrangements with other religions which did allow women. Among these were the religions of Isis and Cybele. It may be that, as the men worshipped Mithras, their wives and children worshipped in the temples of these goddesses.

Mithras had slaves among his followers, and included not only Romans but members of what we would call ethnic minorities. In the light of the times the religion was remarkably tolerant.

Most groups of the time excluded slaves. In this Mithrasism was as notable an exception to the common practice of religions as Christianity. Moreover, Mithras included Romans of ancient family stock as well as recent arrivals. In this the appeal of Mithras was clearly wider than that of Christianity which, until the sixth century, was largely confined to Greek-speaking orientals.

---

[2] See M.J. Vermaseren, *Mithras: The Secret God* (London: Chatto and Windus, 1959), pp. 162-163.

The Many or an Elite?

No direct written evidence survives to tell us how the Mithrasians saw themselves. Did they, as did the Christians, see themselves as the heralds of a new age? Or did they see themselves as the protectors of the status quo, as would befit imperial soldiers? Did they see themselves as a proselytizing religion, seeking mass membership? Or were they content with small numbers, seeing themselves as an elite?

It has been suggested Mithrasian organization could never have been part of a mass movement. I.A. Richmond, in *Roman Britain*, suggests two major reasons for this.[3]

First, the size of the god's temples. These were always small, holding a dozen or at most twenty followers. Second, the demands the god made on his followers were too great to ever gather and hold such a large following. The demands required too much spiritually and intellectually in an age when easier paths were available. But not all writers accept the followers of Mithras had any great demands placed on them. Burkert suggests, in *Ancient Mystery Cults*, little intellectual depth to the religion.[4] Indeed, the word he chooses to describe it is not a religion, but a *thiasos*—a religious association. To Burkert, Mithras offered little more to his followers than convivial gatherings wrapped up in religious trappings.

Any examination of the facts, however, shows that the path of Mithras was arduous indeed. The initiations became legendary for their severity. Many followers abstained from sex. They were required to surrender all accolades to their god. In Rome, where divorce was common, the followers of Mithras were allowed to marry only once. Moreover, they were required to be brave, fearless, upright, scrupulously honest, and truthful. To be a Mithrasic merchant was to be a watchword of keeping one's bargain and providing honest goods for the price.

---

[3] I. A. Richmond, *Roman Britain* (London: Penguin, 1955), p. 209.
[4] Burkert, *Ancient Mystery Cults*. See for example, chapter 3, "Theologia and Mysteries: Myth, Allegory, and Platonism," p. 69.

The followers of Mithras took their oaths very seriously. There was far more to Mithras and his followers than conviviality. But was it all too much for the Roman public?

I think we have to agree with Peter Arnott. In *Introduction to the Roman World* he states Mithrasism and Christianity were different from the other religions of the Empire, exercising a more thoughtful, less spectacular appeal to their followers.[5]

But if Christianity could become a mass religion with its demands, there is no reason Mithrasism should not do the same. With that in mind, let's turn to Richmond's second point: the size of the Mithrasian temples.

The layout of a Mithrasian temple was quite strict. They all had benches on either side of a narrow aisle. Worshippers lay on these benches during celebrations, which included partaking of full meals. No temple yet found could accommodate more than forty or fifty people on its benches. Most would only have held between one or two dozen. From this and the number of Mithrasic temples found, Richmond deduces that Mithrasism never claimed more than a small number of adherents.

We should remember, however, the number of Mithrasian temples found which had been desecrated by Christians as well as the unknown number destroyed or which had new buildings placed over them (the Mithrasic temple under St. Prisca in Rome is an example). Even with this destruction, over a hundred Mithrasic sites survive in the city of Rome alone, with literally hundreds of others throughout the Empire. So in addition to the sites we know we have to query how many others were destroyed, covered over, or remain to be found. There might have been several thousand Mithrasic temples if we include the numbers of villas or homes with a single room dedicated to the god.

But to argue on this alone is not enough. Even if we say there were two thousand temples and stipulate that each held forty people, this would only account for a membership of 80,000—less

---

[5] Peter Arnott, *Introduction to the Roman World* (London: Sphere Books, 1970), p. 284.

than a tenth of Christianity's membership when Constantine chose it as the new Roman state religion.

Historians, however, have made certain assumptions about the use of the temples—assumptions so simple they have escaped notice. Once again, the dominant Christian pattern of worship has been accepted as universal and everything else is interpreted as a variant from it. Certainly Mithrasian temples held only a dozen to two score people. But that is how many people they held on their benches at any one time. Thanks to Christianity (and Judaism), we are used to thinking of worship as occurring on a "sabbath day." But there is no reason why Mithrasians should have chosen one day of the week for worship.

Indeed, Mithrasism's astrological associations would have made it highly unlikely that one day could be singled out as being more holy than the rest. There were seven grades, each associated with a planet. To choose one day as more important than the others would have been a direct affront to those grades associated with the other six days.

Moreover, the merchants and soldiers who were almost certainly the bulk of members would not all have had the same day off. The idea of a universal rest day came from Christian (via Jewish) doctrine. By contrast, a group with occult thinking might have had different groups in the temple on each of the seven days of the week. On Tuesday, for instance, the members of the grade Miles would have their ceremony—Tuesday being associated with Mars and Mars being the planet of the Miles degree. In this way a hypothetical membership of 80,000 becomes 560,000.

Of course the full mathematical possibility of this model could not have been realized in practice. The leader of the community was called the Pater (father) and was associated with Saturn. There would obviously not have been as many Paters in attendance on Saturday as there would be Coraxes (Ravens) on Wednesday (Mercury's day).

The murals of the Sacred Meal show another point. Of all the depictions of the members of various grades, no first degree Corax is ever shown seated. Lions are shown sometimes seated, sometimes standing; but Coraxes always stand, usually serving the other members. Moreover, the food served in the representations of the Sacred Meal appears to be cooked. But with only one or two exceptions, the temples had no cooking facilities. Where was the food cooked? By whom?

I would suggest that the food was cooked outside the temple, probably by those unable to attend the main ceremonies, and brought by Coraxes. Such facilities, assembled around the temple (which was often not a prominent building) would give it the appearance of a small military fort. In fact, Tertullian's[6] comment in *De Corona* that Mithrasians worship a god of light in something which is "truly a camp of darkness" may be more literal than most historians have taken it to be.

In other words, the Mithrasian temples did not, and never were intended to, hold the whole membership at once. What proportion they did hold we cannot tell without textual evidence, which is utterly lacking on this point.

What we can say, though, is Mithrasism almost certainly had a far wider membership than some have been willing to accept. We would be indulging in the worst sort of historicizing to assume the movement was from its inception destined to be an also-ran. Given the probable size of each temple community and the number of temples found throughout the Empire, the membership of the Mithrasian religion would have numbered something over 250,000. This number excludes females and children worshipping in temples of Cybele and/or Isis. If we assume only half the male members were married and of those that were the average marriage produced two children, the Mithrasian religion would have represented something like 625,000 members of the Empire.

The Community

Unfortunately, we know very little about the structure of the Mithrasian community and how the members organized themselves. We

---

[6] Quoted in Vermaseren, *Mithras*, p.38.

know the community was lead by a *Pater* (father) and the members referred to each other as *frater* (brother). And we know that the initiates organized themselves into seven degrees. Beyond that, we have only the testimony of certain events, evidence from surviving murals, and inscriptions from which we can make inferences.

We don't know for instance, how people were approached to become members of the religion. We don't know what they were told about the religion. We don't know what criteria new members had to meet or how they were promoted from one degree to another. We don't even know if there was a limit to the number of people who could occupy any given grade in a Mithrasic temple.

We do know that Mithrasic temples were kept deliberately small, though we don't know why. We know the configuration of the buildings, but we know very little about the people in them. Such knowledge would reveal much about the religion as a whole. Few scholars have attempted to analyze or study Mithrasian communities, feeling it a lost cause in the face of such sparse evidence. But we may be able to reconstruct more of the broad outlines of these communities than we have heretofore realized.

For instance, we know that the followers of Mithras were mainly soldiers, and that the religion had a definite martial character, strongly influenced by the general organizational and religious principles of the Roman legions.

It would seem incredible if martial men in a martial organization should cast aside their careers (terms of enlistment were commonly twenty to twenty-five years) and the religious ethos of the legion to create a completely opposing organizational structure for their religion. It is reasonable to suggest, then, that the structure of Mithrasism would be hierarchical, with orders proceeding from the top down. The lowest degree probably had little to say in the administration of the Mithrasic temple or the religion generally. Their job, like good soldiers, was to serve. In murals we see the lower orders literally serving their superiors. They acted as waiters at the Sacred Meal for members of the higher degrees. It is also likely that the pyramidical structure characteristic of an army was adopted for Mithrasism. That is, there were probably more members in the lower degrees than in the higher: more Coraxes than Leos (Lions); more Leos than Paters (Fathers).

We do have the evidence of a case where the Pater of a temple died, and a replacement had to be sought from a considerable distance away. This tells us several things about the community. A temple of Mithras apparently could not operate without a Pater, probably no more than a Christian parish could operate without a priest. This implies that the Paters were the sole repositories of certain functions or knowledge of sacerdotal or religious significance. The fact that a new Pater had to be sought from the outside indicates Paters were not elected by individual temples. This means there was no internal promotion process for becoming a Pater, which in turn means that there must have been some external, central control of the religion.

It also indicates that there was only one Pater at a Mithrasic temple at a time. This was very much in keeping with the martial character of the religion—an army unit has only one commander. The Pater, filling a similar role, was also singular.

That a Pater was "transferred in" is also in keeping with normal Roman military practice. Shortly after a man was promoted, he was transferred to another unit. It seems likely that a similar procedure applied in the religion of Mithras, at least for members with full-time religious duties.

And finally, the fact that the new Pater would travel a considerable distance to take up his post indicates the position was indeed a full-time occupation. The Mithrasian religion boasted a full-time professional clergy.

Being able to travel a distance to take up an official position also argues that the priests of Mithras were celibate since an individual would be far easier to transport and support than a family. We know that a great many followers of Mithras voluntarily practiced celibacy, and it was in fact illegal for Roman soldiers to marry, a law not repealed until the reign of Severus in 197 C.E., more than 250 years after the religion of Mithras came to Rome. Moreover, in divorce-prone Rome, Mithrasians who could marry could do so only once. So it is likely what the followers *might* do is what the leaders were *required* to do.

The coming of the Pater tells us more about his community. A stipend of any sort indicates a temple had to have finances. Gifts, fees, tithes, or some such must have paid for the various building efforts, the decorations, the support of the Pater, and the other fiscal aspects of the religion. About such finances we know next to nothing. Certainly gifts and votive offerings formed a significant element of the funding of the religion. The food of the Sacred Meals was no doubt provided by the laity and in part consumed by the priesthood.

Probably there was some proportionate imposition of burdens. The relatively large number of offerings from higher officers—who could not have been a high proportion of total membership—suggests this. We can guess the wealthier members donated money and hired the artisans necessary for construction. Poorer members probably donated time or what skills they had. The state offered nothing; the Mithrasian religion was financially self-supporting. That some regular financial arrangements existed is attested to by a piece of graffiti found on a temple wall which shows a list of expenses for wine, beef, and other such items. But Roman accounting generally was rather poor and we know little about the finances of the religion.

The importation of this anonymous Pater also sheds some light on how a member rose through the various degrees of Mithrasism. If the Pater was not elected by or chosen from among the local members, some other authority must have decided who could become a Pater. In fact, graffiti in temples have shown us that a Pater was chosen "pater nominus" by "consacranei syndexi." That is, he was chosen according to law by his brother-initiates: a Pater was chosen by the other Paters, though by how many and by what method is uncertain.

We also know from graffiti at Rome of a more complex sacerdotal apparatus. Remember there were over one hundred Mithrasic temples in the city. In addition to the title of Pater, there was also the title of *Pater Sacrorum* (Father of the Sacred [Ceremonies]) and the title of *Pater Patrum* (Father of Fathers). This latter figure was *de decem primus pater patrum*, indicating that the Pater Sacrorum was chosen from, and perhaps by, a council of ten. He was chosen for his special knowledge—particularly of astrology. Whether his authority was over Rome alone or over the whole religion is impossible to say, though the centralization of military groups favors, by analogy, a universal authority.

But any such military analogy leads us to the question of promotion within the ranks. Did followers, joining at the first degree (Corax) generally expect to rise higher? If so, how high? Surely not all expected to be a Pater, but how many could reasonably hope to become a Leo?

Again, we have to infer our answers to these questions from the murals found in various temples. A careful examination of these murals, however, reveals an intriguing possibility. We see several members of a degree in only two cases: Corax, the lowest grade, and Leo. In the other five degrees, only individual members are portrayed. (There is the single exception of a relief of members of the second degree in what I believe to be a chorus.)

The fact of a single Pater we've already explored: with the exception of the Council of Ten or perhaps in gatherings in the larger cities, there appears to be only one Pater per congregation. But this doesn't explain the representations of single members in other degrees. In reliefs of the Sacred Meal we see one Pater, one Heliodromus (Sun-runner), several Leos, several Coraxes, but only rarely a Perses, Nymphus, or Miles—and then only one of each degree.

Where we do see other degrees, it is often in a sacerdotal role, or engaged in activities which represent their attributes. For example, a picture of a Perses (Persian) shows him with a stick bringing fruit down from a tree—the Perses degree being said to be the "keeper of fruits." In the same way we see other degrees during their initiation. A mural of a Nymphus (Bride) will be used to show the attributes of the degree, as at St. Prisca in Rome and at Ostia. I think this provides the major clue. Mithrasian degrees were not symmetrical. Members did not follow a pattern of slow incremental development through each degree, as in the Golden Dawn. They might spend a great deal of time in a lower degree and then rapidly climb up the scale to another plateau, rather like the modern Masons.

A new member first became a Corax and remained one for a long time (there were no doubt exceptions—like an Emperor or two). If they appeared to have the potential to become a Leo, they passed quickly through the intervening stages of Nymphus and Miles. The training was intense and the scrutiny close and harsh. Hence there would be a large number of Coraxes, a rather smaller membership in groups of the next two degrees, and then a larger group of Leos. The picture is complicated somewhat by the Nymphuses, who may have formed a kind of choir for the temple. If so, there may have been as many as a dozen Nymphuses per temple, most of whom would rise no further.

A similar pattern occurred at the next stage. Members remained Leos for a long time, in most cases for the rest of their lives. Given the nature of the Pater's role, it seems likely that only the single, celibate, or of independent means would rise to the position of Pater.

That alone would leave many with Leo as the highest degree they could attain. This degree parallels the Royal Arch rite of the Freemasons and the Adeptus Minor degree of the Golden Dawn, though it was in many ways a much more difficult degree to attain than either of these. Its attainment was proof of extensive study of serious occult arts, not its inception.

Again, the murals tell the story. There are few representations of members of the Perses or Heliodromus degrees. Those that survive show them in a ceremonial role. Like the Pater, they wear distinctive clothing and have allotted functions in different ceremonies. This may indicate that, if a Mithrasian rose higher than Leo, he did so through clearly defined ceremonial or perhaps administrative posts. This would be in keeping with the military nature of the religion and its worshippers. Officially a commandant of a unit is its sole ruler. In practice he normally has a staff who carry out many of the individual administrative functions of the unit. It seems likely the Pater had one or two aides-de-camp to carry out administrative duties.

Ceremonial duties, as well. Historians often forget ceremonies must be impressive if they are to stir the deepest waters of the soul.

To depend on the oratory or presence of a single person in all temples to Mithras would have been suicidal. Religion does not fare well for very long on "one man shows', and the Romans followed Mithras for about 600 years in the highly charged atmosphere of Rome.

It was imperative the ceremonies be impressive. When a group is concerned with ceremony to such a degree the officiants must know their parts by heart—cue cards take away some of the atmosphere! Those most concerned with ceremony in recent times, such as the Freemasons and the Catholic Churches, have the same view.

Where roles must be learned by rote it indicates a regular set of participants and a regular pattern of presentation. In the case of Mithrasism it appears that the Pater, the Heliodromus, and the Perses learned their roles by heart.

So from among the Leos the Pater would choose a few who would take the higher positions and a Heliodromus to act as vice-leader of the community. When an opening came up, a Heliodromus would become a Pater. To do this, he would have to pass those tests of knowledge portrayed in the graffiti on the walls of the Mithrasic temples. Such an opening would only occur on a Pater's death, resignation, incapacitation, or defrocking. Alternatively, the community of the temple might grow large enough to allow the group to split into two. In that case, the new community would need a Pater, as well as a new Perses and Heliodromus.

Thus it was to the benefit of members seeking promotion to convert as many new members to the religion as possible. If the temple split, there would be at least three promotions, possibly more. In this way the Mithrasian religion inevitably became a proselytizing religion. But quite how they gathered new members has not really been understood.

What we can do is look at other groups with similar interests to the Mithrasians and look for possible parallels. The means of organizing human affairs may be many, but they are not infinite. If we can find the parallels we may understand more about the nature of the Mithrasian religion.

I have chosen four organizations: these are the Hermetic Order of the Golden Dawn, the Freemasons, the Knights Templar, and Christianity.

The Golden Dawn

The Golden Dawn is a magical order founded in 1888. It had a vitality no other organization of its kind then or since has been able to match. Its membership included some of the most important occultists of modern times, among them S. L. MacGregor Mathers, Dion Fortune, W. Wynne Westcott, W. B. Yeats, Algernon Blackwood, and Aleister Crowley.

The technology of its magic of the Golden Dawn was of a high order. In fact, many occultists consider anything originating from the Golden Dawn to be definitive even today.

There are some striking parallels between the Mithrasian religion and the Golden Dawn. Not the least of these is the practice of correspondences which both organizations brought to a pinnacle of sophistication. Both organizations were inclined to secrecy. In the case of the Golden Dawn, this secrecy extended to the very existence of the organization. The Golden Dawn was known however, in those circles from which it would be most likely to draw potential candidates for membership—suitably mysterious publicity and word of mouth ensured that.[7]

Like the Mithrasians, the Golden Dawn had a system of degrees, although one that was much more complex than the Mithrasian's encompassing up to fourteen degrees of initiation, some of which were not open to mortal human beings. What really separated the Golden Dawn from contemporary groups was its use of correspondences. In this the various elements of color, number, words of power, geometric figures, and many other items all interlinked with each other and with the spiritual realm.

---

[7] Though the Golden Dawn had a maximum membership at any one time of perhaps 300, compared to the minimum thousands of Mithrasians, such publicity is wide enough for comparison.

So aggression is attributed to Mars. Mars is also associated with the color red, the number five, the five-pointed star, and so on. Joviality, of course, is associated with Jupiter. Jupiter is associated with blue, four, the square and so on.

By this system, the Golden Dawn derived a complex pattern of spiritual exercise and development. Each degree of initiation, for example, can be associated with certain principles such as a planet, an element, a spiritual virtue. In this initiation, from one degree to another, reflects the spiritual nature of the universe. Like the Golden Dawn, each degree of the Mithrasian religion was associated with a planet, a constellation, and certain religious or moral principles. Like the Golden Dawn, these spiritual values had physical analogues in colors, numbers, and elements. The Mithrasians developed this type of system of correspondences more fully than any other group in antiquity. In this I compare the Mithrasian religion to Isis, Christianity, and even the gnostic movement.

To have developed such a system, and to keep it secret, led the initiates of the Golden Dawn to a sincere belief that they were an elite. I suggest the same belief developed among the Mithrasians. Both organizations developed from a milieu. The Mithrasians emerged from the religious fervor of the Roman Empire, the Golden Dawn from the orientalism and Freemasonry of the late nineteenth century. In both cases much of what the groups held secret existed in that milieu but in an unconnected form.

For example, the Golden Dawn taught its initiates the Hebrew alphabet and linked its symbolism to that of the Tarot. Both these traditions were known in the culture at large, and a well-read candidate would have known almost the whole of the lessons of the early degrees. What the Golden Dawn teachings did was to draw these disparate concepts together in a new context and give them special meaning by attaching them to the grades of initiation.

The Mithrasian religion did much the same. People could look in the sky and see Leo; they knew the planets; they knew fruitfulness was good and barrenness was bad. What Mithrasism did was to draw these disparate elements together in a new and meaningful way.

Once we understand that we begin to understand how the Mithrasian religion could recruit new members. There was much that could be revealed without giving away anything at all. A prospective Mithrasian could be told "we are a mystery religion," "our teachings demand high moral standards of our followers," "ours is a god of light who battles against the darkness," "we teach a special form of astrology." This is exactly the kind of detail the poet W. B. Yeats records receiving, when he was asked to join the Golden Dawn.

The emergence from a milieu further explains why Mithrasian membership tended to show certain characteristics. The Golden Dawn emerged from the Freemasons and the Theosophical Society. Its membership maintained similar qualities ever after. The Mithrasian religion, emerging from soldiers, maintained that martial quality. Only those who came in contact with soldiers—merchants, nobles who often took military office as part of their careers, etc.—became members in any great numbers.

The Knights Templar

But several differences also pertain between the Golden Dawn and Mithrasism. The Golden Dawn did not rest on martial foundations—though one of its leaders tried to make this so. The Golden Dawn claimed to be an academic or spiritual elite. For a Roman soldier, preserving an Empire and at times deciding who would be Emperor, the concept of being one of an elite was far more palpable. The Mithrasian's role as guardians brings them closer to the Knights Templar, an order formed to protect pilgrims traveling to the Middle East.

The elite nature of both the Mithrasians and the Knights Templar was recognized by outsiders. Both groups were widely known in the communities in which they lived. While few people knew of the Golden Dawn, most people knew of the Templars and the Mithrasians. I stress it does not matter whether the Templars had anything like secret practices or doctrines of their own. The parallel is with military organizations which gave themselves an elite status through religious duty. Like the Mithrasians, the Templars placed their swords and shields in the service of their deity, backing this up with a rigid practice of discipline, prayer, moral standards higher than those of the general community, and arduous regimens most contemporaries did not have to pass through.

The Templars wore plain tabards and armor in stark contrast to the colorful attire of the times, claiming their god alone deserved fine raiment. Similarly, at the initiation to the degree of Miles, the candidate had to push a proffered laurel wreath away with the words, "My god is my victory." Ever after he could not accept a wreath of victory. Mithrasians and Templars alike refused the normal rewards of their societies. This denial could only heighten the sense of duty of individual members.

To strip rewards away is to place heavy reliance on discipline, and such a discipline must be greater than that required of contemporaries.

Templars were forbidden to retreat unless outnumbered by at least three to one. They lived by a stringent pattern of monastic life. Similarly, Mithrasian merchants were noted for their honesty, while Mithrasian soldiers were proverbial for their bravery. Templars were obligated to say numerous prayers each day, were denied marriage, and had to refrain from speaking for any reason other than necessity. Mithrasians also labored under numerous restrictions, although the nature of these is not fully known.

Both Templars and Mithrasians were trained to endure physical hardship as part of their regimen. Mithrasians suffered themselves to be bound (possibly gagged), blindfolded, manhandled, and even imprisoned in something about the size of a covered bathtub. The Templars were accused by Philip le Belle, the King of France, of similar practices and were known to put their members through physical privations such as fasts and meditations. These disciplines were more than other knights were asked to endure.

Like the Mithrasians, the Templars made their decisions in secret conclaves. Not only were outsiders barred, but members of their own order were not allowed to know the deliberations of their leadership. I believe the Mithrasians had a similar method, and this is one reason we have so little knowledge about the religion's administrative apparatus.[8] But the parallels between Templars and Mithrasians help us reconstruct how the religion was administered. If we do not know detail, we can guess broad outline.

We have seen that the Pater was at least nominally responsible for the promotion of members, at minimum to the degree of Leo. And we know that he had at least two regular assistants, sometimes three. Since it is likely that, during the service of the Sacred Meal matters of business, finance, promotion, and discipline were discussed, he probably had to contend with the advice of his Leos as well.

But the Pater was responsible to a central authority which appointed Paters to individual temples and replaced them in the event of death, incapacity, or inability. This hierarchical structure continued up until it reached the Father of Fathers. Elected at Rome, the Father of Fathers was not simply a local leader but a universal one. In this he would parallel the Master of the Templars.

The Master (the title Grand Master was only used after the suppression of the Order) was the unquestioned leader of the Templars except that he was subject to his own council.

At other levels the leader of a unit was responsible, through a hierarchy, to the Master and was advised (like the Master) by his own aides and the nobles under him. In the event of unsuitability for any reason, a leader could be replaced.

The leaders were monitored by representatives of the Master who could audit accounts or question members, and replace leaders if necessary. A similar group must have existed within Mithrasism.

This group would have travelled from temple to temple to ensure that all was well. This would not be a frequent visit, but its existence alone must have done much to maintain the administrative network.

---

[8] This is more than the general paucity of textual evidence. Had Christianity collapsed I think we would have learned far more about how it had been run because its deliberations were open to the whole membership.

Like the Templars, such centralization meant that some place had to function as a nominal capital. For a religion enmeshed with the Roman Empire, that place could only be Rome. Thus the Father of Fathers must have wielded a universal authority.

The similarities between the Templars and the Mithrasians are striking. Yet one major difference distinguishes the two. The Templars were not an initiatory body. Although they had levels, or ranks, (knight and serjeant (sic)), they had no degrees or grades. All parallels are administrational. To find parallels between two widespread, publicly known initiatory bodies we will have to compare the Mithrasians to the Freemasons.

The Freemasons

Comparison between the Freemasons and the Mithrasians has been frequent. The groups shared a number of obvious traits: both exclusively for or at least dominated by men; both were secret societies which kept their teachings at least officially secret; both were initiatory bodies with degrees conferred for esoteric learning; both publicly upheld high moral standards; both held a strong attraction for soldiers and merchants. But there is another similarity between the two groups which has been missed. Both represent stages in a wider continuum of religion.

Freemasonry does not in fact claim to be a religion but rather an enhancement to its members' own religions. It has thus always sought to avoid (and deny) the notion that membership in a Masonic lodge is incompatible with individual members' religious practices. Mithrasians included the symbolism of Greco-Roman mythology in their temples. There are murals of Oceanus, Saturn, and Jupiter. But these figures only observe what Mithras is doing or act without Mithras present. Both groups present themselves as something traditional but also as something new. Both rest heavily on the reputation and prominence of their members to sustain a reputation when the detail of their teachings is to remain secret. The Mithrasians had a great many members from the Roman nobility, just as the Freemasons have many patrons from the British nobility. Civil servants and clergy have also been prominent in both groups. Both recruit from all ends of the social scale, but enjoy a significant number of members who hold important, though not necessarily prominent, administrative or business positions.

Thus, although Freemasons and Mithrasists presented doctrines outside the societal norm—the myth of Mithras and the myth of Hiram—neither rejected their society, and both worked to develop links with existing traditions.

Masonic lodges frequently specialize in the type of person they recruit. In London, for example, there is one lodge which recruits exclusively from the police. Lodges also specialize in which part of the Masonic doctrine they implement. Some lodges are almost purely social, others are ceremonial, while yet others are esoteric training schools. In this Masons are fundamentally different from the Golden Dawn. The latter was bound to a single goal. When Mathers attempted to introduce additional goals to the Golden Dawn, he precipitated a split from which the Order never recovered.

I believe the same thing occurred in Mithrasic temples. Though some elements were standard, different temples gave emphasis to different aspects of the religion. The temple at Aventine, for example, must have been a special training area. Since it is in Rome this would be in keeping with the idea the Pater Patrum had been an especial student of astrology but had also been chosen from among a council of ten. I think this council was especially concerned with teaching new Paters the secrets of the religion.

Masonry and Mithrasism centered on a number of goals and showed the diversity in their organization. But here there is a fundamental difference between the organizations. Where Freemasonry may have initiates who are themselves members of the clergy —particularly in the United Kingdom—there are no Masonic clergy per se. By contrast, there is evidence of at least two cases in which Mithrasian Paters were specifically brought in to perform the sacerdotal duties of other religious bodies. One was a priest of Isis (whose own name was Mithras) and the other was the last

Hierophant of the Elysian Mysteries, both of whom were Paters of Mithras.

This possession of an organized priesthood gave Mithrasians a prestige Freemasons have never attained. They also became enmeshed in the society to a greater extent than the Freemasons. Did the Mithrasists' success arouse opposition? It does seem the success of Freemasonry (enjoying between four and six million members worldwide) coupled with its secrecy has resulted in hostility. Some authors have complained about the potential for abuse when they have no examples to cite or can only make vague accusations. The same complaint could with equal justice be laid at the door of sporting associations. They, too, have a prominent membership spread across the social spectrum. The significant question for us here is whether Mithrasism came to grief through its secrecy as did the Freemasons and the Knights Templar. To discuss this question, we need to compare Mithrasism to its nearest rival, Christianity.

Christianity

The world was not predestined to be Christian. In fact, even after centuries of military and cultural domination, Christianity is neither the largest religion in the world (Buddhism is), nor the fastest growing major religion (Islam and Bahai are both growing faster). Nor has it come to power in any nation through conversion alone, as has Buddhism in southeast Asia. Christianity has succeeded only where the central authority has been converted first and where it has had the opportunity to suppress rival religions by force.

Yet historians continue to apply an unwritten rule to the history of Christianity—every rival which differed in structure or theology was at a disadvantage because of that difference. What is more, all too often the Christianity under consideration is not the system as it existed then, but the system which exists now. This is far from the case. Christianity has undergone many changes, made many compromises, over the centuries. If there are similarities between Mithrasism and Christianity today, these were even stronger in the first four centuries of this era.

Theologically, the religions have many similarities and parallels. Writers of the time certainly considered the two rival and similar creeds, not opposing doctrines. These similarities caused Christian polemicists much difficulty. Some accused Mithrasism of imitating Christian ideas and ritual. But Mithrasism in its Roman form had emerged a century before Jesus was supposed to have been born. Forced to acknowledge this, other writers said the Devil, knowing the form Christianity would take, created Mithrasism first in order to denigrate those sacraments. This same pattern of accusation, admission and new accusation was made against Buddhism and the religion of Isis.[9]

Until the fourth century, Christianity presented itself as another mystery religion. It wasn't until 313 C.E. that the First Council of Nicea met to discuss the nature of Jesus. Until that time, many churches accepted him as no more than an enlightened teacher, while others worshipped him as wholly divine and without physical existence. The composite creed which issued from this Council—that Jesus was fully human and fully divine, and God the Son—was decided by a show of hands, a close majority engineered partly by the bribes of the Emperor Constantine and partly by the weapons of a few Imperial guards.

But, in the early years, the similarities between the "mystery religion" of Christianity and the cult of Mithras were striking. Instead of small wafers and a sip of wine, Christian worshippers brought full loaves of bread and jugs of wine, much closer to the Mithrasian Sacred Meal.

New converts would be sent from the Church during the final part of the ceremony, the mass of Catuchemas, in which bread would be turned into flesh and wine into blood. They were considered unworthy of the miracle to come.

---

[9] C. M. Daniels, "The Role of the Roman Army in the Spread and Practice of Mithraism," in *Mithraic Studies*, ed. John R. Hinnells (Manchester, England: Manchester University Press, 1975), p. 315.

There were no cathedrals in these early years—the term "cathedra" actually only means "chair" and came to mean "seat of authority." The early Christian churches were small, the size of a temple of Mithras. In Rome, the Mithrasic temple of St. Prisca was adjacent to a Christian church of the same size. That church was run by a matron, the St. Prisca in whose honor the basilica which stands on the spot today was built.

Even iconographically the two had similarities. That is, in many ways Mithras was shown similar to the Christ being shown then: Both were portrayed as young and beardless; both were sometimes shown in a shepherd's role; both were noted for a sacrificial deed by which we were saved. This theological similarity should not surprise us. I have described how Mithrasism came to the West when Cilician pirates were settled in Greece in the first century B.C.E. One of the major cities in Cilicia was Tarsus. Paul of Tarsus came from Tarsus some 180 years after the Cilician pirates had been resettled. He may well have been influenced by the sacerdotal currents of the area.

Both Mithrasism and Christianity recruited from a wide spectrum of society. We mustn't forget the radicalism (in Roman eyes) that Mithras would let slave and Emperor worship together. Nor that the grade system meant a slave might outrank a nobleman within the religion. Christianity recruited more from the "foreign" elements: Etruscans, Greeks, Greek-speaking merchants, Egyptians, and other people once perhaps independent in their own empires, but now subject to Rome. The Mithrasians also recruited among these foreign groups, but they also converted many of native Roman stock. Unlike the Christian god, Mithras made peace with the gods of the Roman pantheon, allowing conservative aristocratic Romans to convert to Mithrasism without abandoning the Empire which they (correctly) saw as a source of stability and learning.

The one great difference in recruitment was Christianity accepted women more than Mithrasism did. The Christian church of St. Prisca—next to the Mithrasic temple—was, after all, run by a woman. In fact, this has been cited as one reason why Christianity triumphed over its rival. But early Christianity was certainly able to dump the feelings and role of women as soon as it gained Imperial patronage. The Christian portrayal of divinity was as exclusively male (or male-ist) as that of any religion in the Empire. Its later condemnations of women and women in religion negates any superior claim in this area.

What Christianity *did* do was to offer an easier path. Like Freemasonry, Mithrasian seems to have believed in salvation through upright action and moral benefice. Christianity preached faith. It promised the murderer, the rapist, and the lecher that they could all enter heaven if only they believed. It was not a religion for the courageous or the stalwart, but for the desperate. And Rome was crowded with the desperate in the first four centuries of this era. Christianity's triumph came when the western half of the Empire was already collapsing. In the ensuing disarray, high moral standards and virtue did not stand many in good stead.

Mithrasism sought to save the world of Rome. To this end, it applied its knowledge and expertise, seeking to purify traditions, and force a stricter moral order on a crumbling society. Christianity, by contrast, rejected the world of Rome. It did not consider Rome worthy of preservation. It aspired to a different, a heavenly, city. Mithrasism could not survive the double blow of the collapse of Rome and the rise of the Christian church.

Chapter 3

The Mithraeum

A temple of Mithras is known as a "Mithraeum" (plural Mithraea), which means "place of Mithras," just as the word museum means "a place for the muses." Throughout the length and breadth of Imperial Rome, the general layout of Mithraea was consistent enough that archaeologists can now determine the ruins of a Mithraeum by its floor plan alone, although, as in any general rule, there were variations and exceptions.

Mithraea were built underground. They were generally small structures, consisting of a long, narrow chamber with a central aisle, lined on either side by a high bench on which members lay during the sacred meal. The building was oriented east-west, with the entrance and often a narthex of sorts at the western end. Here officiants probably robed themselves in their ritual vestments.

At the eastern end was a nave holding the altar or altars. Here stood the icon of the bull-slaying scene. This last item was the central image of the religion—more important by far than the crucifix or the chi rho monogram to Christianity. If there is any modern parallel, it is to the tracing boards of the three degrees of Freemasonry. In addition, there were niches for statues, murals, reliefs, etc. As in Christian churches today, these decorations differed from Mithraeum to Mithraeum.

We don't know why Mithraea were kept small. Some scholars have suggested that the small size of the building indicates a small membership. But there is every reason to discount this theory. At times not only nobles but actual Emperors of Rome patronized the

Mithrasian religion. Even if the overall number of members had been small there would have been plenty of money for large, impressive structures. Some small masonic lodges for instance, have had impressive quarters thanks to the gifts of wealthy patrons. Moreover, there are over a hundred temple sites in Rome itself. Even if limited membership had enforced small units elsewhere, here at least, one would expect to find larger structures. But even in Rome, the largest Mithraeum could hold, at best, about fifty people. Likewise the one Mithraeum known to have been built above ground, in London, was also of modest size. The size of the group must have been theologically significant.

Or more correctly, of occult significance. Esoteric rites seem to derive power best from modest-sized groups. Extremely large groups cause a diffusion of power. Very small groups have less aggregate power. The size of Mithraea may have been calculated to provide the ideal milieu for controlling numbers to maximize occult power. Moreover, in a moderate-sized group, each individual member had a chance to participate in the temple's rituals and could be counted upon to know their part in the ritual. Ceremonially oriented groups find memorization of script vital to maintaining the atmosphere of the ritual. In the Zarathustrian religion, priests are expected to memorize rituals and execute them faultlessly. Since Mithra was a god of that pantheon, Mithrasians probably held the same view.

Both the Golden Dawn and the Masons expected perfect execution of ritual. Members working private rituals could use prompt cards in the Golden Dawn, but this was considered inferior occultism, certainly not suitable for public ceremonies like the Corpus Christi ritual. Likewise Freemasons insisted that their officers know their rituals, and much time is spent making certain every officer knows their part by heart. To fail in this was considered a serious breach of protocol at least, and magically ruinous at worst.

Like its size, the floor plan of the Mithraeum probably held some doctrinal significance or ritual purpose. The pattern of a long central aisle flanked by high benches in a long narrow building seems to have been germane to the activities of the group. The

London Mithraeum, for instance, maintained this characteristic design even when it was in no way necessary. In fact, only one example of a variant design survives—the Mithraeum near Ponza, which contains a relatively wide central chamber.

The benches, called "praesepia" or "cribs," were used by members to recline, not sit or kneel. The Sacred Meal would be eaten in this position. This arrangement was also characteristic of Greek symposia. But normally symposia were held in a room in a house. Couches thus did not flank a central aisle, but were more likely grouped around the center of the room.

It is possible, of course, that we are faced with a bias in the remains we have found. We should remember Christians, when they got the chance, desecrated Mithraea. They burned them, hacked them with axes, dumped corpses from graveyards in the chamber, blocked the entrance way with garbage, and physically attacked and killed members of the group.

In such circumstances it may be suggested what has survived has largely been those underground structures. Others, easier targets, were destroyed. Certainly an unknown number of Mithraea consisting of a single room in a large house have been lost. These may have shown greater variation, if only by practical necessity.

It is significant, however, that even in those known of exceptions to the characteristic design, very little was changed. The London Mithraeum was built above ground, but it still consisted of a stone chamber with the same layout of benches on either side of a central aisle. The structure near Ponza was wider than usual, but built in the same scale and with the same aisle-bench-nave construction as others. This indicates that what remains of the Mithraea is what the Mithrasians themselves preferred, and thus must have had meaning to the Mithrasians: When necessity forced a variation, the Mithrasians not only tried to maintain all other characteristics, but recognized the variation *as* a variation.

That such architectural consistency was preserved throughout the Empire and over centuries strongly suggests the religion had a central authority. That authority maintained the architectural rules because they had meaning. Surviving evidence seems to support the deliberacy of underground construction. The Mithraea were often decorated with pumice to give them the appearance of caves and the terms used to describe them in ancient writings— "speleum," "specus" and "spelunca"—all refer to caves. Another term used to describe the temples was "crypta," which also indicates an underground structure. The "cave" symbolized the cosmos. The Mithraeum may thus have represented a miniature of the universe, acting as a symbol of the cosmos as a whole. Their ceilings were often decorated with gemstones; sometimes holes were bored through the ceiling, positioned to allow the light of certain stars to penetrate at a certain time and on a certain date each year.

The Golden Dawn used a similar structure called a vault. This chamber consisted of seven wooden panels forming walls, and a wooden floor and ceiling. The whole was painted symbolically. Occult power from rituals performed in the vault was said to remain in the vault itself. The cave-like design of the Mithraea may have served a similar purpose. Stone construction (used even in the London Mithraeum) has long been held to conserve occult power—note Stonehenge, ancient menhirs, and the pyramids. The ritual power of the Mithrasians may have been enhanced by stone construction. By meeting in a symbolic stone miniature of the universe, they may have developed their magical energies and tailored them to their own theological needs.

As mentioned, the Mithraeum was normally oriented east-west, with the magical focus in the east. In Caesarea Maritima there survives a remarkable example. The Mithraeum was built with two scuttles or skylights. The western one let in light to fill the antechamber. The eastern one was apparently positioned to allow a ray of light to rest on the altar at noon on the solstice. The symbolic importance of this is reinforced by a series of holes across the arch of the ceiling in the eastern part of the Mithraeum. It would seem wooden beams were placed in these holes, which, if the beams maintained a constant width over their whole length, would have met in the center of the Mithraeum in the image of a rayed sun.

Mithras was a god of light, and the architecture of his temples reflected this. The Mithraea were underground not, as the

Christian writer Tertullian alleged, because they were "veritable camp[s] of darkness."[1] By building underground, the Mithrasians could control how and when light was admitted. Just as a hungry man appreciates food more than a sated one, so light is better appreciated in darkness. The Mithrasians could not create enough light to overwhelm the day but, by shutting out most light, that which remained took on its true character.

It is also true that in darkness people have a heightened sense of expectation. The Golden Dawn, the Freemasons, and the Templars all blindfolded their members at some point during their initiations. In doing so, the Golden Dawn and the Masons specifically stated that the candidate was being shown they were in darkness and were seeking light. The Mithrasians no doubt had the same principle in mind in their use of light.

The moderate size of the Mithraea provided little space for ritual activity. The Mithraeum at Heddernheim, for example, has an apse which measures roughly eighteen-and-a-half by five-and-a-half feet (6 x 1.8 meters), and an aisle which measures twenty-seven-and-a-half by six-and-a-half feet (9 x 2.1 meters), including the stairs at the apse. Taking into account that much of that space would be obscured from the view of someone reclining on the benches, that leaves an effective "stage" of only about thirty feet by seven feet (10 x 2.1 meters). At Ponza, the widest known Mithraeum measures about twenty feet by thirty feet (6.5 x 10 meters), but for a part of that twenty foot length, it measures only about twenty-one feet wide (6.9 meters). Moreover, the length includes a cult niche just over six feet deep.

Though these sizes are not small enough to be cramped they do lead us to certain conclusions about the kind of ritual likely to be performed there. The perambulations used in Freemasonry, the Golden Dawn and the Zarathustrian religion for instance, were

---

[1] Quoted in M. J. Vermaseren, *Mithras: The Secret God* (London: Chatto and Windus, 1959), p. 38 The expression seems to have been overlooked by later writers, who tend to avoid *De Corona* as a source altogether. Certainly some of his comments are difficult to reconcile with fact, but he was writing of a secret group of which he was not a member.

probably not practiced in the Mithrasian religion. Much more prominent would be processions or two-person rituals, both of which occur in a number of murals. Also significant would be rituals which could be performed while stationary. Prominent among these are confrontation (e.g. challenging a candidate), communion, and the Sacred Meal, all of which appear in the murals found in Mithraea.

Actions by members on the benches would also be limited. Rising from or returning to the benches frequently would have been inconvenient. If headroom was not a problem, then certainly the need to step over a plate of food would have been. The Pater more likely made a statement to which the audience gave a ritual response. Epithets of the god, and terms like "nabarze," and "nama" (Persian for "holy") would have to be among the responses given.[2]

The rest of the structure of the Mithraeum would have various elements of symbolic import. For example the central aisle consisted, in some cases of compacted dirt, as at Ponza and Caesarea Maritima, and in others of a mosaic, as at Ostia, where the floor mosaic gives the degrees in order and the attributes of each degree. Compacted earth was in most cases probably not symbolic but inexpensive. One exception to this assumption survives at the Aventine Mithraeum, the largest ever found. Here there are three side rooms off the central area described by Vermaseren as being the ritual homes of three of the four elements—the one with a clay floor obviously being the room of the earth. We know that the degree of Leo (Lion) was associated with fire. It would be remarkable if the other elements were not also associated with degrees. If so, both the Mithrasians and the Golden Dawn used the same

[2] The word "nabarze" occurs in some inscriptions in relation to Mithras. Cumont assumed it to be of Persian origin and to mean "victorious," largely because other epithets of the god indicate victory. Another suggestion is that "nabarze" came from the Old Persian "na brzah," meaning "high or great male." This interpretation is based on epithets given to martial gods. But though Mithras was followed by soldiers, he himself never takes the field against an army, or faces an obvious enemy. Within the context of the inscriptions, it is possible that "nabarze" is occult power. Occult numinosity was an attribute of Mitra, Mithra, and Mithras.

motif for lower degrees, though the two groups were separated by about 1700 years and probably had a different order for element and degree.

Ritual Statuary

Votive objects have been found in a number of Mithraea. Among the most important, and perhaps the most misunderstood, are the statues of the so-called "lion-headed god." This figure tradition-ally takes several forms, but most commonly that of a human fig-ure with a lion's head. Around its naked body twines a snake, the snake's head resting above that of the lion.

Cumont and Vermaseren claim that this statue represents Aion, the god of infinite time who, in Persian literature, is called Zervan. Zaehner, a scholar specializing in the religion of Zarathus-tra, believes the statue to represent Ahriman. More recently Ul-ansey has suggested that the figure is the gorgon Medusa.[3] He points particularly to similarities between the statues and a sixth century B.C.E. Attic vase painting of the gorgon with a human-ani-mal face with lion-like attributes, and a statue in which the lion-headed god has a gorgon's head on its chest (the figure on the chest could also be a lion). Ulansey suggests the statue represents the power of Mithras to overcome his enemies, just as Perseus (the model for Mithras) overcame Medusa. In this case, however, a cos-mic power is attributed to Mithras.

With all due respect to these individuals, though they are not-ed academics not one of them is an occultist. They cannot see what an occultist would see. For there to be both a degree Leo (Lion) and a lion-headed statue must indicate a connection between the two. It is obvious enough that if connection were denied rupture would have occurred in the group.

Some Masons, on reaching the Royal Arch degree, are dis-

---

[3] David Ulansey, *The Origins of the Mithraic Mysteries: Cosmology and Salvation in the Ancient World* (Oxford: Oxford University Press, 1989) p. 117.

turbed by revelation of the word "Jahbulon". This is not indicated in the first three degrees and many find the syncretism of the degree disturbing. It has led to resignation and revelation of Masonic secrets.

Had such a rupture occurred in Mithrasic circles the Christians would certainly have preserved a record of it.

To understand the statues better, we have to realize they are not all lion-headed, and that what appears great inconsistency between them reveals a significant and, once it is understood, obvious meaning. The statues are a representation of the Leo degree as internalized. It is an esoteric key to the concept of adeptship among the Mithrasians. In all initiatory bodies there is an "adept" degree. At this level, the student has mastered the lessons of the group and internalized them. The student has become one of the teachers, but more important has taken the next step in human evolution. The many statues are representations of this state. Though the statues differ in many ways, the lessons they teach remain the same.

South of the Alps, the lion-headed god is portrayed in statuary as a human figure with a lion's head, entwined by a serpent. The figure stands on a globe which often has two bands around it. In either hand he holds a key; over his heart is a small lion's head. Either two or four wings sprout from his back, or sometimes from his hips or lower back. Sometimes the body is covered with the signs of the zodiac. North of the Alps, however, and in the Danube area, no lion-headed figure has ever been found.

In statuary found in German areas, by contrast, the figure has a human head. In some cases, instead of a lion's head over the heart, there is a thunderbolt. But the other elements—keys, globe, and signs of the zodiac—remain. A snake still entwines the figure; he may still hold the staff. These are not two similar figures but two versions of the same figure.

In one statue found at Castel Gandolfo, the figure has a lion's head, but no serpent entwines it. Instead of a lion's head over the heart, there is an eye, while lions' heads appear on the stomach and the knees. A breach clout covers the figure's genitalia, which are normally covered by the snake. In another case the serpent has been shattered to bits by the figure who wears Persian trousers. (We will examine this figure more completely when we discuss the Leo degree in chapter 5.)

Occultists have long accepted the belief that the body contains certain centers of power. It seems clear the Mithrasians saw this power—this nabarze—as centered in the head, heart, and genitals. Some Mithrasians would apparently add the throat, stomach, knees and feet.

The lion-headed god showed this power and defined its character. That is why there are certain variations in the statues. This power so developed allowed the person who could control it—the Leo or the adept—to perform certain magical acts. This would naturally include the magical blessing of food, the charging of talismans, etc. But more importantly, this power could liberate the soul, setting the initiate on a path back to the source of things, bringing them to the verge of being able to stand separate from the world. The statue stands on a globe encircled with two bands— one representing the zodiac, the other the celestial equator. He holds the keys to the heavens (the same keys that now appear on the Papal flag). Thus the Leo is in direct communication with the divine powers that command the lesser mortals of the world.

Statues of figures other than the lion-headed god have also survived: in the Mithraeum at Sidon (in Syria), a statue of the triple goddess Hecate; in the Aventine Mithraeum, a head of Serapis; in the Mithraeum under the St. Prisca, a triple-headed bust of Hecate with a bowl on her head; elsewhere, statues of Venus, Saturn, and others.

This variety of statuary indicates the Mithrasians, like the Knights Templar and the Freemasons, saw themselves as part of the continuum of ancient mythology. Unlike the Golden Dawn or the Christians, the Mithrasians did not see themselves as irreparably separate from their world.

Other statues are specifically Mithrasian. A number of statues have been found of the Sun-god, of Mithras, and of his torchbearers. Mithras himself has been posed as a figure riding horseback, slaying the bull, and being born from stone. In one statue found at Rome, Mithras emerges, not from a rock, but from a pine cone. Since pines are a symbol of immortality (their hermaphroditic nature makes them self-generated), this implies that Mithras, too, was considered self-generated.

In the many representations of Mithras' birth, he holds a number of different objects. He almost always holds a knife in his right hand. If this is intended as the blade with which he will later slay the bull, it indicates that his action was one of destiny. His left hand holds variously a torch, ears of grain, or a globe of the world. The torch indicates he is to bring light to the world. The ears of grain refer to fertility and possibly the Rite of Eleusis, whose last priest was a Mithrasian Pater. The globe indicates Mithras' dominance over the world.

Murals and Reliefs

Murals give us a major portion of our knowledge of Mithras. They provide the bulk of bull-slaying scenes, the heart of the religion. They also depict initiation ceremonies, the events in Mithras' life, processions, officers, and details of the degrees. Murals at the Mithraeum at Dura-Europas in Syria give a marvellous insight into the religion. Surrounding the central icon is a remarkable and well-preserved series of panels which show Mithras as an archer on the sacred hunt, with Sol in the Sacred Meal, and the war between Jupiter and the Titans.

Another panel shows a Pater seated on a throne. He is dressed in Persian garb. In his right hand is a staff or cane, in his left a scroll, indicating that the Pater's authority depended at least in part on the written word. This suggests dependence on some central text, contradicting the argument put forward by Walter Burkert in *Ancient Mystery Cults* that Mithrasism possessed no sacred literature, only practice and ritual.[4]

[4] Walter Burkert, *Ancient Mystery Cults* (Cambridge, MA: Harvard University Press, 1987), p. 69.

Several representations of Cupid and Psyche survive, dating from about the second century C.E., suggesting that *The Golden Ass*[5] by Lucius Apuleius may perhaps have influenced the Mithrasian religion. In *The Golden Ass* the hero is turned into a jackass. Through various adventures, he comes to hear the myth of Cupid and Psyche, which is recounted in the book in full. Through that myth, his attitude toward women changes, and this in turn leads to his salvation and inclusion in the religion of the goddess Isis. The hero is then initiated into the mysteries of Isis, then Osiris, and then Serapis. Since heads of Serapis have been found at Mithraea and a Pater of Mithras took a position as priest in the Isisian religion, it is quite possible that this book, read extensively in the classical age, may have influenced the Mithrasian religion.

One intriguing archeological find is a marble relief of three equilateral triangles set concentrically. Within the central triangle is a crescent Moon on its back. As the fifth degree (Perses) was attributed to the Moon, it seems likely that this is some kind of degree badge. No such badge survives for the other six degrees, although it is possible that the one for the Heliodromus was a circle in a single triangle. Moreover, we don't know how such badges might have been used, though the possibility of them functioning as astral keys suggests itself. Unfortunately the surviving clues are frustratingly scant.

Gems and Talismans

Various gems have also been found in Mithraea. They may have served as amulets, much like the gnostic gems that have been found, or like the crosses and chi rho monograms of Christianity. But they may also have fulfilled a more magical purpose. Many of the gems

---

[5] Lucius Apuleius, *The Golden Ass*, trans. Robert Graves (London: Penguin, 1950). Chapters 7 to 9 give the legend of Cupid and Psyche, in which the hero's altered perception of and treatment of women marks the turning point in the story. This feminist interpretation of the story, though, does not occur to Graves, who in the introduction attributes the change to the notion that bad luck can be acquired.

in fact portray bull-slaying scenes. Since the bull-slaying was the magical focus of the religion, it may be that the gems were meant to reflect that icon. Thus the magical energy (nabarze) would flow from the greater to the lesser receptacle.

These talismans were sometimes scaled to the size of the raw material used and hence don't always carry the many minor figures common to the central icons themselves. One, a marble medallion found in the Mithraeum at Caesarea Maritima, however, shows a rather complete scene. Mithras stabs the bull, and on either side of him are the torchbearers Cautes and Cautopates. Below this scene are two other events in Mithras' life: his birth from stone and his hunting.

Some gems add new figures to the familiar bull-slaying scene. On one gem, apart from arrows or palm leaves of victory, there are magical figures like a Greek cross in a rayed sun, and other more abstract images. Another gem shows Mithras being born from stone. On either side of Mithras are the *dioscuri*, minor figures of Greek mythology sometimes thought to be connected to the torchbearers Cautes and Cautopates. Above Mithras, a phoenix holds a worm or serpent; below him appear the wine and bread that formed the Mithrasian eucharist about half a century before Jesus was said to be born.

A Temple Interior

Let us take a walk through the interior of a typical Mithraeum, as it might have been when Mithrasism was at its height. The temple, oriented from east to west, is built underground with only a long roof with an air chimney and some holes visible from above. You enter from the west, walking down the steps into an anteroom, where officiants robe themselves for their parts in rituals, and where candidates await their ordeals.

The building is 6.25 meters (about nineteen feet) wide and 15 meters (over forty-nine feet) long, making it neither the largest nor the smallest of Mithraea. Its anteroom is about 4 meters (about twelve feet) long, perhaps a bit larger than most. It is not very high, constructed as a single arch with a maximum height of just under 4 meters (over twelve feet). The walls are straight with a near-circular arch at the ceiling. This is the roof seen from outside.

The anteroom is walled off, with an open doorway into the main hall. Since you are entering a holy place, there is probably an altar here for you to show your respect. (Some Mithraea have altars, others statues.) On the walls on either side of the door, there is a painting in stucco of the torch-bearers of Mithras, Cautes and Cautopates. Cautes is wearing bright yellow and his torch is pointed up. Cautopates is in blue-gray and his torch points downward. Around Cautes is a springtime scene, and around Cautopates a scene of autumn. Each scene shows a tree, the first in full flower, the second heavy with ripened fruit. Both figures stand with one leg crossed over the other; each carries a bow in his free hand.

As you step through the door, on your left is a statue of Mithras being born from stone. This was his first miracle, and by seeing it you take the place of the shepherds who viewed the original miracle. In his right hand, Mithras holds the dagger with which he must slay the bull. In his left, he holds the globe of dominion. On the globe are two bands, representing the zodiac and the equatorial belt of constellations. Perhaps a genuflection is appropriate here. No occultist, no student of the mysteries, no religious person, would pass that statue without a mark of respect.

You can not take long, however, as there are people behind you. Perhaps you trace in the air before the statue the badge of your rank. Perhaps you trace a religious monogram, such as the cross on the bread of the Sacred Meal. Or you may simply pray or repeat an epithet of the god. You may say, for example, "Nama Mithras, deus genitor rupe natus," meaning, "Holy Mithras, the god born from the rock."

That done, you continue on into the Mithraeum. On either side of you are raised platforms, the "praesepia" or cribs for the celebrants.

May you sit anywhere? Or were members' positions fixed, perhaps by rank? We don't know, but the large number of soldiers in the membership makes it likely that each member had his place. Because of the inconvenience of jumping up to the crib, the members probably filed in in order, those who filled the first positions coming first, those who filled the last places entering the room last. You are the first, so your place is the first seat on one side of the far end of the Mithraeum. This gives you a fine view of the interior of the building and all it contains.

Despite Tertullian's taunt that this is a "camp of darkness," the Mithraeum is illuminated by oil lamps,[6] allowing you to see everything in detail. The arch of the ceiling is painted azure. Precious stones or cut glass are placed to give the impression of a night sky. There are holes bored through the ceiling, too. On certain nights these holes line up with and admit the light of certain stars.[7] In this Mithraeum, certain fixed stars of the zodiac shine through. When the lamps are extinguished, only the light of these stars illumines the tiny cosmos. Only their spiritual energies enter and are meditated upon. It is a profound moment.

On the floor is a mosaic. Like the one at Ostia, it shows the seven degrees with their attributes. Just at the door is a large panel showing a serving dish—a mixing vessel with two cups. To the right stands an altar with a fire leaping high, reminding you of the companionship expected of members. All your arguments are left outside these walls. All grudges are here forgot, as is all ambition and rank. So the officer-Corax serves the slave-Leo with the deference truly due his rank.[8]

As you cross the mosaic, you walk along the separate grades of initiation, each set off from the others by a kind of ladder of rungs. First is the Corax represented by a raven (Corax is Latin for Raven), a cup, and a caduceus (the staff of Mercury). Next

[6] A cache discovered near the Aventine Mithraeum indicates as many as sixteen lamps could be used at once. For a small space, this would provide excellent illumination.

[7] At Caesarea, in Syria, a Mithraeum was built which only let the sun shine on the altar on the days of the equinox.

[8] Mithrasism is very different from other religions of the Empire in this respect. In the traditional state religions, the rank of secular life carries over into sacerdotal duties. In other cases, members are drawn only from the slaves, or only from the officers, but not from both.

comes Nymphus, the bride. This panel shows a bridal veil with a diadem, a lamp, and perhaps a mirror.[9]

The next panel gives the attributes of Miles, the soldier. His symbols are the soldier's kitbag, the lance, and the helmet. Then comes Leo, the adept's degree, in which a Mithrasian enters fully into the secrets of the religion. Leo's symbols are the thunderbolt of Zeus, the sacred rattle or sistrum, and the fire shovel.

Next is Perses. His symbols are three in number as well: a crescent moon with an eight-pointed star between its sidelong horns, a scythe, and a sword with a hook, much like the one Perseus used to behead the gorgon. Following Perses is the Messenger of the Sun, Heliodromus. His symbols are the torch, the seven-rayed nimbus or rayed headdress, and the riding whip. And finally you come upon the Pater, the symbol of the community and the only degree to have four devices rather than three: a ring, a staff, the Phrygian cap he wears, and a sickle.[10]

At the top of the mosaic is a final panel bearing the dedication of the man who left money in his will for its construction, replacing the compacted earth that had been the floor. It contains his name, a solicitation, and, below that, a funeral urn with some sprigs of acacia around it.

Taking your place on the right-hand side, you can see the various panels and decorations on the wall. Since the degrees come under the protection of the planets, it is not surprising that these murals show the signs of the zodiac. Just below the arch, the various zodiacal signs have been painted with a blue ribbon connecting one to the other. The signs are staggered. As you enter, Virgo is on your left, and Libra on your right; then Leo is on your left and Scorpio on your right; and so on. So, from the east of the tem-

---

[9] The mosaic at Ostia is damaged, obscuring the third item. But since a painted figure at the same Mithraeum is holding a mirror, we can guess that this was also the third item in the mosaic.

[10] If the staff and ring are taken as a single device (and their positions indicate they may be), then there are indeed only three devices for this degree as well. Probably, as for a Christian bishop, the ring and staff are joined. And the ring no doubt bore a signet with which letters to the Aventine Mithraeum could be sealed. No academic has mentioned this pattern of three.

ple looking west, on your left are Aries, Taurus, Gemini, Cancer, Leo, and Virgo. On your right are Libra, Scorpio, Sagittarius, Capricorn, Aquarius, and Pisces.

Behind the cribs themselves, set into the walls, are niches in the form of recessed arches, as at the Mithraeum in Sofia. Within these are paintings showing the life of the community and reflecting the feats of the god. There are four panels on either side, set opposite to each other. As you walk up to your seat, on the left is Saturn handing the thunderbolts to Jupiter. Between them is an altar, indicating the treaty by which the rule of the universe or office of kosmokrater was handed to the younger god. Thus did the golden age of innocence and naivete end. It is a reminder to all members that Mithras is a god of the changing of the ages. Thus did Ouranous give way to Saturn, Saturn to Jupiter.

The right-hand panel shows a Pater seated on his throne. He wears Phrygian style hat, and a Persian tunic and trousers rather than a Roman toga or military leather-strap kilt. In his right hand, he has the cane of office, and on his finger, the signet ring of this Mithraeum. In his left hand, he holds the scroll containing the liturgy of Mithras.

There is no single accepted liturgy. Certainly the rituals, passwords, symbols, astrological calculations and much of the other material is the same throughout the Empire. And all books have the life and deeds of Mithras recorded. But sometimes Platonic material is included as in the *Republic*, the *Timeus* or the *Critias*. At other times Cicero's *Dream of Scipio* is included. Still other Mithraea use the Yast of Mithra from the *Avesta*, the book the followers of Zarathustra use.

The left-hand panel of the second pair shows Sol and Mithras at the Sacred Meal. Mithras holds a drinking horn, Sol holds a bunch of grapes. Before them are the small loaves of bread with the cross on them. Behind and between them are the Phrygian hat of Mithras and the nimbus of Sol, combined together so that the nimbus shines around the hat. There are seven short rays and twelve long rays to the nimbus.

On the right is the community's Sacred Meal, with the Leos in the Mithraeum being served by the Coraxes. A Pater and a

Heliodromus take the place of Mithras and Sol. Around them are all the other grades. The Nymphus has on a veil, the Miles a soldier's helmet, the Corax and the Leo have been given heads like those of their namesakes, and the Perses wears a Phrygian cap with the badge of his grade on it.

In the third pair of panels, the left-hand side shows Mithras ascending to the heavens in Sol's chariot. Sol is by his side; Mercury flies next to them. Below them is the world, and in the distance, just by the horizon, Luna drives her chariot into the underworld. On the right side is a unique painting of the ascent of souls. It shows the stellar and reincarnationist beliefs inevitable to the religion of Mithras.

The painting shows the Milky Way as a ladder of stars. On it the souls of humanity ascend and descend. As Plutarch revealed to the world, the proper seat for Mithras is the equinoxes, for he is the god of the middle.[11] He is the judge of souls, for by shedding blood he has given all humanity the chance of eternity.[12] The tropic of Cancer is the northern gateway through which souls enter into the world; the tropic of Capricorn is the southern gate through which they leave. The Moon, Luna, is attributed to the tropic and sign of Cancer as the planet closest to us. Saturn, the farthest away, is attributed to the tropic and sign of Capricorn. So the painting shows the two paths of the zodiac from Cancer to Capricorn.

Halfway along the cribs are two niches. In one stands a statue of what some call the "lion-headed god," a statue which represents the grade of Leo and all that its teachings imply. This statue is placed in this position to show that it is at this stage that the frater is faced with his greatest test on that path between Cancer and Capricorn.

In the other niche is a statue of three-headed Hecate: she is virgin, lover, and crone. She is set on a central axis with each of her three faces looking toward one of the three points of an equilateral triangle. Below those faces, but looking toward the sides

---

[11] Michael P. Speidel, *Mithras-Orion: Greek Hero and Roman Army God* (Leiden: E. J. Brill, 1980), p. 43.
[12] Vermaseren, *Mithras*, p. 83.

of the triangle, are three whole figures of Hecate, again as virgin, lover and crone. The "korb" or bowl on her three-faced head shows the fruitfulness and blessing which all three faces ultimately bestow. For together, Hecate is all women as men see them, containing the hopes and fears, the light and darkness, the freshness and exhaustion to which all born of women are heir.

Finally, at the far end of the Mithraeum is the apse, where the two altars and the sacred image are held. All other symbols in the Mithraeum derive from this. The altars are double cubes, but with a capital and a base added. The corners of the capitals are set at the corners of the cribs, the edges of which define the apse. On the front of the left-hand altar is the figure of Sol. He stands naked except for a short red cape. There is a whip in his right hand, a globe of dominion in his left. The globe has two bands on it. Behind him are several trees.

The altar on the right shows Luna. She too has a nimbus on her head, but with seven rays rather than twelve. She is dressed in a blue toga. Under her right foot is a crescent moon with the two horns uppermost. In her left hand she holds an infant; in her right she holds a long stick with which she can beat down the fruit in the trees behind her.

In the back of both altars are niches for storing ritual implements. Behind the altars in the apse is the bull-slaying scene. Above all else, this represents the meaning of the religion. It is that which holds it all together—the cosmic event that provides salvation for so many throughout the Empire.

Chapter 4

The Icon
in the East

The bull-slaying scene is the center of the religion of Mithras. It defines the religion more closely than the crucifix, the Star of David, and the crescent define Christianity, Judaism, and Islam respectively. A more accurate comparison would be to the Golden Dawn's use of the Tree of Life, or perhaps to the tracing boards of Freemasonry.

In fact, the Golden Dawn had other symbols to reflect the Order. But the Tree of Life was the central concrete representation of the philosophy the Order taught, all of which was related back to this one glyph of ten circles and twenty two lines. Similarly, Masons use tracing boards, flat boards painted with a number of interconnected images. One is brought out for each of the three degrees of regular Freemasonry. As a member passes through each degree, he is presented with a board. The individual items are pointed out and explained. Though they appear ordinary to the uninitiated, the candidate learns the occult or moral value of each item.

A very similar importance attaches to the bull-slaying scene of the Mithrasians. This scene, like the tracing board, was a representation of the moral and occult values to be found in the Mithrasian religion. Like the glyph of the Tree of Life, the bull-slaying scene was meant to encompass the whole of the religion's teachings. There is no writing as to what the symbol meant or even what the Mithrasians themselves called it. Modern scholars have simply called it the Tauroctony—which is Greek for "bull-slaying scene."

Whatever its meaning, the image stood at the very heart of every Mithraeum. It was set in the back of the nave, at the end farthest from the door, so that it dominated all proceedings. It was the central influence of all the religion for over five hundred years. Many examples of the Tauroctony have survived. They range from small versions inscribed on semi-precious stones (perhaps as talismans), to murals several meters square, to statues in bronze and stone. With so many representations remaining it is not surprising that some variation exists in what was represented and how. We should compare the variations in the Tauroctony to the many variations in the crucifix. There are, for example, the Latin and Orthodox crosses, as well as the Greek, Maltese, and Iron Crosses. Some of these forms have a human figure on them; some do not. The ends of the cross are sometimes decorated with embellishments, and sometimes not. What would an archaeologist make of these variations if it had been Christianity which had lost?

Some of the differences in the Tauroctony may be a function of the materials used in their construction. It would have been impossible, for instance, to include all the elements of the scene on a talisman the size of a coin. Some variations may reflect artistic temperament—outside artists were sometimes brought in to decorate a Mithraeum. But in all cases the membership knew what was essential in the image and could recognize its power, just as Christians know the cross refers to the crucifixion whether there is a figure on it or not.

One might think with all this there would be general agreement, then, on what the image meant. Unfortunately there isn't. Not only is there no text to tell us, the various Tauroctonies are entirely without graffiti. A mute testimony to their importance and the veneration in which they were held.

But that said, we are now closer to understanding the meaning of this symbol than ever before. When we look at the ideas of the academics we will add to their researches the skills of occultists. We will find this quickly peels away the veil of allegory to show the true meaning of the symbol.

Tauroctony

The Mithrasian bull-slaying scene is the only symbol of a religion which consists of an entire scene rather than an abstract symbol or single item. Its central image portrays Mithras stabbing the neck of the bull near the shoulder. Without this central image the other elements of the scene are not recreated in their respective roles. They may play other parts but they do not appear in common roles.

In this image, Mithras always stands above the bull. The stabbing is never depicted as an act of desperation, but rather as an act which occurs after Mithras has established his superiority over the bull. Thus Mithras always rides the animal's back; the animal always has its legs folded; the bull is never standing. With his left hand, Mithras holds the bull's head back, usually by the muzzle, but occasionally by one horn. It is always the right hand that plunges the dagger, and always at the same place.

Mithras always has his left knee rammed into the bull's back, pinning it. His right leg is stretched out, his foot on the hoof of the outstretched rear leg of the bull. Sometimes the god's foot is near the animal's hoof. But the bull's leg is always extended. There are some small representations in relief which have the bull with his legs under him, but they seem to be examples of variations due to the limitations of the material.

There also survives a bowl (possibly to hold consecrated bread) which shows Mithras almost riding the bull side-saddle. His knee is not rammed into the bull's back, but his right foot still hold's down the bull's rear right hoof. And though his knee is not in the bull's back, Mithras still bends the left leg as if to pin down the bull. The portrayal may well be a function of the shape of the bowl.

Mithras always turns his head away from his own action, a pose which deviates from the general canons of classic art. As Ulansey[1] points out, another major example of such deviation, is found

---

[1] David Ulansey, *The Origins of the Mithraic Mysteries: Cosmology and Salvation in the Ancient World* (Oxford: Oxford University Press, 1989), p. 30.

in representations of Perseus, who cannot look directly at the gorgon as he beheads her. There is, however, a minor precedent for this. Prometheus, chained to his rock, looks away from the eagle which each day eats his perpetually regenerated liver. Since Mithras has a saddened look on his face as he performs the deed, it is possible that regret makes him turn away. Alternatively he may be looking at some of the other figures in the Tauroctony.

The bull himself bleeds from the wound in his neck. Sometimes this is ordinary blood, but in some portrayals sheaves of wheat gush from the wound. In others blood flows from the wound, but the tip of the bull's tail has turned into wheat. Sometimes the tail shows two sheaves; more frequently it shows three. Mithras' right foot holds down the bull's hoof consistently enough for us to consider it significant. Possibly he is preventing the bull from pulling in his leg in order to stand. But he may be preventing the bull from fending off the scorpion that always appears just below the bull's genitals. Every known Tauroctony, from Heddernheim to Rome to Dura-Europa, shows the scorpion in the same place. Indeed, the Heddernheim scene, which has the bull raised from the ground to permit the placement of other figures, shows the scorpion raised, too. Furthermore, not only the vertical position of the scorpion, but also its proximity to the genitals, appears to have been significant. The scorpion always holds the bull's penis or testicles in its pincers.

Another subsidiary figure depicted with a high level of consistency is the dog. This is always placed in front of the bull, on its hind legs, its forelegs resting against the bull's neck. Eagerly, joyfully, it laps at the blood pouring from the bull's wound.

Three other main figures fill the lower part of the picture—the lion, the mixing bowl, and the snake. These figures tend to vary much more than the the dog and the scorpion, and are less consistently displayed in both position and stance. The snake is usually shown in the wave-like pattern classical artists used for serpents generally. Although it is always shown below the bull, its position varies widely. A relief from Secia (near Damascus) shows the snake headed left, near the bull's genitals, next to the scorpion. In the mural at Capua, by contrast, the snake faces right, as it does in most representations, but its head is nowhere near the bull's genitals. Rather it is shown just outside the knee of the bull's forward buckled right foreleg. And where the body of the snake at Secia is quite short, at Capua it extends for a greater length than the bull itself.

Yet another relief and a statue of the Tauroctony, both from Rome, show the snake seeking out the wound in the bull's neck. It seems, like the dog, to be lapping up the blood from the wound. But in other murals, the snake does not seem to seek the bull at all. In a relief from Heddernheim, the snake is entering or looking into the mixing bowl. This same position is repeated in a relief at Osterburken. In a relief at Fellbach, the snake entwines the bowl once and then turns to look into it.

Images of the lion and the mixing bowl are even less consistent than those of the snake. They may not appear at all and, while there are instances where the snake appears without the lion or the bowl, there are no instances in which either the lion or the bowl appear alone. In all cases, however, the bowl is a two-handled mixing bowl; the lion is always male; and the two are always placed in relation to each other.

The lion often appears on a clearly smaller scale than the rest of the picture—possibly to indicate that it is a mortal figure in a landscape of gods. In the relief from Osterburken, for example, the bowl rests on its base with the lion next to and looking at the bowl. The lion is the same height as the bowl and is, in fact, smaller than the dog shown in the same relief. The lion is under the bull's right foreleg hoof; the bowl is to its left.

The relief from Neueheim shows the lion and bowl in the same, reduced scale. But the bowl is in front of the bull's right foreleg knee. The lion is above it, looking on the scene with some apparent fear. A bronze plate from Brigetio again shows the lion looking at the bowl, but this time the lion is standing. The snake's head is above the bowl; the bowl is under the bull's right foreleg knee; the lion fits under the bull's left foreleg. In one case, the lion performs a kind of handstand over the bowl.

To the left and right of Mithras are his torchbearers, Cautes and Cautopates. These two figures are miniature versions of Mithras himself. They have the same face and the same style of clothing. Cautes points his torch up; Cautopates points his torch down. The way the torch is held differs in small details. The relief at the Louvre shows the torches being held in one hand. The relief of Campo Santo (Pise) shows the bearers holding their torches in both hands. The mural at Capua shows different coloring for each figure. Cautes is in yellow trimmed with green, with red cap, cloak, and boots. Cautopates is in gray with violet showing in the folds of his costume.

The figures of Cautes and Cautopates are often shown with their legs crossed, as at Heddernheim. At Capua, however, they are shown walking or standing. The crossed legs will be familiar to occultists from the Tarot cards World and the Hanged Man. It is interesting, on this point, that at Heddernheim, Cautes is shown with his left leg over his right; Cautopates with right leg over his left. Where the torchbearers are included (and they are not invariably included), and are crossing their legs (which they do not always do), they always have this pattern of left over right and vice versa.

The figure of Mithras himself looks over his shoulder rather than at the deed he is committing. He is looking at a ray of light, a raven, or both. One or both of these figures appears in all but the smallest of Tauroctonies. The raven is sometimes perched on the ray of light, as at Capua. In other cases it perches on a cloud, the outer facing of a cave wall, or Mithras' own cape (as at Heddernheim). In the relief of Osterburken, the raven sits on a stone in an outer panel which frames the Tauroctony itself. But in no case is the raven actually shown flying.

Behind the raven in a large proportion of cases, and the source of a ray of light in all cases where he appears, is Sol, the Sun-god. This figure is common in Mithrasian art and appears in a reasonable number of Tauroctonies. Sometimes only Sol's head is shown, sometimes a torso, and sometimes the whole figure. Capua, for example, shows the head and torso. Sol holds his riding whip, has his usual short red cape, and appears to be naked. In the relief at the Louvre, Sol is shown as a full figure riding his horse-drawn chariot. In the relief of Campo Santo, Sol is only a head wearing a nimbus, emerging from some clouds. Directly opposite Sol in this relief is the head of Luna. She wears a veil and surmounts a crescent shape. Wherever Sol and Luna appear together, however, they are always similarly portrayed: if Sol is a bust, so is Luna; if Sol rides a chariot, so does Luna.

In addition to these central figures, a number of minor elements may appear in a Tauroctony, although these do not always appear or appear in any consistent manner. The background to Mithras' actions, for instance, is often a cave or a cloud. The first symbolizes the universe, the second the ceiling, or limit, of that universe. Together they represent human life as contained, but capable of liberation.[2] At times trees are placed in the background of the Tauroctony—behind Cautes, they tend to be trees in spring, behind Cautopates, they tend to be trees in autumn. The signs of the zodiac also appear in a number of Tauroctonies, forming an arch over the scene, as in the mural at Dura-Europa, or surrounding the entire scene, as in the superb marble relief at Sidon. Sometimes these zodiacs flank various side panels showing scenes from the life of Mithras and/or the life of the community, although these are purely ornamental and not a part of the iconography of the Tauroctony itself.

Interpreting the Tauroctony

The Tauroctony is the richest religious symbol in human history, providing a wealth of icons and images to anyone attempting to determine its meaning and significance. Yet scholars have been unable to arrive at anything approaching a consistent interpretation of Mithrasian symbology. The available scholarship tends to fall into two main categories: the textual and the astronomical—although this latter is itself divided into a number of competing views.

Early writers, like K. B. Stark,[3] noted that some of the elements of the Tauroctony also existed as constellations. His com-

---

[2] Plato's analogy of the cave in *The Republic* is an example of this concept.
[3] See Michael P. Speidel, *Mithras-Orion: Greek Hero and Roman Army God* (Leiden: E.J. Brill, 1980), pp. 6-7.

parison, however, was limited—Canis Major was associated with the dog, Hydra with the snake—and involves only minor figures in the scene. Stark suggested Canis Minor as the prototype of the dog, but carried his analysis no further.

By contrast Franz Cumont related the various figures, not to constellations, but to the religious literature of Zarathustra and the Persians. But Rome and Persia were deadly enemies, and as recent writers point out, this might have prevented Rome from worshipping a Persian god, and discouraged any type of theological exchange.

This modern view, paralleling American-Soviet or Allies-Axis animosities, ignores the fact that in the ancient world, the clergy was often allowed free access through enemy lines, as were traders. Total war as we know it did not exist. Governments fought each other, leaving social intercourse and civilian populations largely undisturbed. Moreover, it was Roman practice to specifically pray to the gods of an enemy nation. When fighting Carthage and its famous general, Hannibal, the Roman Senate offered the Carthaginian gods greater temples than they already enjoyed if only those gods would give Rome victory. When Rome did win, the Senate kept its promise.

Table 1. Two Sets of Constellations.

Speidel	Ulansey	Image in Scene
Scorpius-Libra	Scorpius	Scorpion
Hydra	Hydra	Snake
Corvus	Corvus	Raven
Virgo-Spica		Ears of wheat
Crater	Crater*	Mixing Bowl
Leo	Leo	Lion
Orion	Perseus	Mithras
Taurus	Taurus	Bull
Canis Minor	Canis Minor	Dog

* Ulansey also suggests that the mixing bowl may not refer to Crater but to Aquarius the water bearer.

But there were problems with Cumont's approach as well. He associates the snake with the fiendish spirit, Ahriman, and the dog with Ahura Mazda. Thus the dog and the snake should be deadly enemies. Yet the image itself does not show them as enemies. They are never shown as hostile to each other—in fact, they rarely seem even vaguely aware of one another.

Dismissing Cumont's, textual approach, Speidel and Ulansey have returned to Stark's astronomical theory, but they came up with somewhat different reasons for the choice of constellations and therefore somewhat different groups of constellations. Most importantly, Speidel concludes that Mithras is Orion; Ulansey argues that he is Perseus. Table 1 gives the two sets of constellations.

Although Speidel and Ulansey agree here on several items, their justifications for their conclusions differ markedly. Speidel[4] observes that, in ancient times, Scorpio was portrayed holding the scales of Libra, while Virgo held Spica, the ear/s of wheat. Moreover, he suggests the images of the Tauroctony correspond to the constellations visible at one given time along the celestial equator from Taurus to Scorpius-Libra. He cites the Farnese globe, an ancient globe representing the sky seen from a "celestial" rather than from a "terrestrial" vantage point.

Ulansey[5] on the other hand, argues that the religion of Mithras developed in response to the discovery of the precession of the equinoxes in the late 1st century B.C.E. About every two thousand years, the sun appears in a different sign on the first day of spring. In 4000 B.C.E., the sun was in Taurus; in 2000 B.C.E., in Aries; at the dawn of the Christian era, in Pisces. In the next millennium, it will be in Aquarius. Like Speidel, Ulansey claims that the images of the Tauroctony depict those signs which lay along the celestial equator as it was 4000 to 2000 B.C.E. Much the same description

---

[4] Speidel, *Mithras-Orion*, p. 10.
[5] Ulansey, *The Origins of the Mithraic Mysteries: Cosmology and Salvation in the Ancient World*, pp. 82-87 give the essential argument.

as Speidel. But Ulansey carries the argument another two thousand years back in time and ties it to this celestial progression.

All three of these theories have their own problems. Speidel, for instance, does not explain why the founders of the religion changed the name of Orion to Mithras. It seems to have been no more than a monstrous deception. As if, after years of learning, loyalty, and effort, an initiate would be happy to be told "Surprise, it was Orion all the time."

It takes more than a pretty pattern tied to a series of stories to sustain the development of a religion. To function as a religious symbol, the Tauroctony had to be tied to an eschatological myth: something showing the struggle between good and evil; something to stir the deepest parts of the human soul. Nothing less would have sustained so many people for over half a millennium.

Ulansey's theory, which ties Mithrasism to a discovery that shattered all current worldviews could account for some kind of philosophic response to the mysteries of the universe. But Ulansey does not provide an explanation for how that sense of wonder at the mechanisms of the universe translated into an eschatology. He fails to explain how the concepts of honor, justice, and sacrifice came to energize the Mithrasian religion into a unique whole, and why new knowledge of the precession of celestial ages should invoke new concepts of individual judgment and moral rectitude.

That the Tauroctony is essentially a representation of certain constellations seems clear from the images of the icon, and the names of the Mithrasian degrees. What no academic has sought to explain, and perhaps none has even noticed, is how the images of the Tauroctony fit with the degrees of the religion: the crow in the Tauroctony, the constellation Corvus the crow, and the degree Corax or raven; the lion of the icon, the constellation Leo, and the degree of the same name. The wheat of Spica-Virgo likewise relates to the degree Nymphus, the bride, and astrologically changes the zodiacal sign of "the fruitful virgin." The bull's wound sometimes bleeds wheat; sometimes his tail turns into grain. The constellation Canis Minor, the dog in the icon, and Miles, the "guard dog" are all related symbols. And the statues of the lion-headed god, which we know represent the adept degree, have a snake entwined about them, indicating the constellations Leo and Hydra.

So there is reason to explore possibilities. But before we begin we should take note of the different possible origins of the Tauroctony: text and constellations.

If the origin was any kind of text—Zarathustrian *Avesta* or otherwise as Cumont claims—then the degrees would come before the images of the icon. By contrast, if the constellation theory is correct, the icon was in existence before the degree system.

No evidence survives of a degree system in the Mithrasian communities in Germanic areas. The closest approximation appears on a bronze plate found at Heddernheim, which shows the seven planetary deities at the bottom. The plate does not, however, include the names of the degrees or their attributes, and the deities shown appear in a different order then that of the mosaic at Ostia. The degree system in fact reached its full flower only south of the alps, at Rome and nearby Ostia. They were of much less concern in the Danube region and possibly in Syria as well. This may show us the way into a theological division within the Mithrasian religion. There are a number of iconographic differences that split along the Alpine divide. Because the degrees appear only in some cases and the icon is universal, the icon came before the degrees.

It therefore must be accepted that the Tauroctony does relate to certain constellations. The beginning of Mithras reasserting his right to head a religion came first from a vision. The constellations formed the backdrop, not a reinterpretation of texts. Hence Mithrasism is a reformation, rather than a heresy. Though it may be grounded in the *Avesta* in the same way the *Avesta* is grounded in the Iranian pagan tradition, its central vision is as different as the Christian notion of Christ is from the Jewish notion of a messiah.

But, as academics have not noted, not all the figures of the Tauroctony had equal importance. Mithras and the bull were central to the matter. The second group, though, consisted of the scorpion, the dog, the raven, and the snake. The third and last circle contained the lion and the mixing bowl.

This is why individual elements of the scene are reproduced even in fine detail throughout the Empire, while, others exist with considerable variation. Various layers, each representing a set of constellations, were added at different times and in different places.

This is characteristic of occult groups, Driven by an initial vision—for example a dream image or a mystic experience—the group then expands on that image, interpreting every experience in its light. As the process continues, new elements accrete to the original. What was a single image encompasses more and more, becoming an increasingly rich agglomeration of symbols, ideas, and methods. Those added later will naturally have less universal support than the original and will vary more in their use and distribution.

This is exactly what happened in the Golden Dawn, in which the paths of the Tree of Life represented the primary symbol. Eventually the Sepheria attracted the attention of Florence Farr, who formed a sub-group within the Golden Dawn called the Sphere Group.[6] This sub-group followed the pattern described above; it gained less than universal support and its existence tended to encourage yet further variation.

Likewise Masons originally had no Royal Arch degree. Its introduction caused enough dissent that Masons began referring to it as the "perfection" of the third degree, deferring to the ancient rules which say Freemasonry has only three degrees. The distinction between a degree and a perfection, however, is moot at best, and even today the Royal Arch is not universally endorsed by Freemasonry.[7]

---

[6] Ellic Howe, *The Magicians of the Golden Dawn: A Documentary History of a Magical Order 1887-1923* (York Beach, ME: Samuel Weiser, 1972), pp. 250-251.

[7] And the variations in its ritual and theology are somewhat greater than that of orthodox Masonry—or rather they were until changes in the last thirty years have begun to fragment regular Masonry as a whole.

A Vision Splendid

A graffito from the Santa Prisca Mithraeum tells us that, by shedding the blood of the bull, Mithras saved us: "And us have you saved by shedding the eternity-giving blood."[8] The constellation Taurus is one of two associated with the bull. Ursa Major, though called the Bear, was sometimes considered a bull. Ursa Major contained the Pole Star of ancient times.

But the bull of Mithrasian iconography sheds blood, indicating that Taurus, and not Ursa Major, was intended. For Taurus actually does shed "blood," in a sense. The path of the Milky Way flows straight through Taurus, who thus "sheds the blood" by which Mithras saved all humanity. In the Roman world, the Milky Way represented the celestial pathway of souls. Souls being born came in through the sign of Cancer and left through the sign of Capricorn. The Milky Way formed the path.

Moreover, the Milky Way contains Scorpio at its farther end. Thus a familiar grouping emerges between the celestial equator and the Milky Way: Taurus, Canis Minor the dog, Hydra the snake, Leo the lion, Crater the mixing bowl, Corvus the raven, Leo, and from Virgo, the star Spica the wheat ear. Part of Gemini also reaches into this group. And, about two thousand years ago, both Orion and Perseus appeared here, partly touching the Milky Way path. Hence, not only the image of the Tauroctony, but something of its theology, can be reconstructed through these constellations.

At an unknown time, probably no more than a generation before Pompey's victory over the Cilician pirates, an individual or small group had a vision. It is probable that this vision came to one already theologically or philosophically trained. It may be, as Ulansey believes, that this vision was triggered by the discovery of the precession of the equinoxes. Until then, the outer sphere of stars had been thought immutable, turning in splendid and divine

---

[8] M. J. Vermaseren, *Mithras, The Secret God* (London: Chatto and Windus, 1959), p. 177. This is a quote from graffiti in the St. Prisca Mithraeum at Rome. The same graffiti is translated slightly differently in Speidel, *Mithras-Orion*, p. 45.

order every night, year in and year out. A change in perception of
this divine order could well have been devastating. But we should
remember the special indication it would bear for a priest of the
religion of Zarathustra. Certainly there must have been insuperable, even violent sacerdotal currents in Cilicia. How else do we explain the Mithrasian religion, Apollonius of Tyana—the so-called
"pagan Christ"—and Paul of Tarsus, all from the same area in a
period of about one hundred fifty years?

We must remember the Iranian pagans saw the sky as having
been made of stone by the gods—Zarathustra in fact said it was
made of stone by Ahura Mazda. The heavens were meant to be immutable, as unchanging as the rest of creation. Change of any sort
in the celestial order, even down to the rising and setting of the
sun, was the work of the fiendish spirit. Since Mithra was already
known to the Iranians as the god who protected the sky—the god
of holy fire and the early morning—they naturally linked this
change in perception to him.

Iranian paganism already contained a myth of the sacrifice of
a bull, attributed to the fiendish spirit, Ahriman. The good result-
ing from the sacrifice in the Zarathustrian liturgy is entirely acci-
dental. Most writers have assumed that the existence of this myth
would have prevented the transfer of the symbolic act to Mithras.
But if a crisis of faith had already occurred, as seems apparent,
many elements of the existing myths might be reformed. With the
attribution of change in the heavens to Mithras, the sacrifice of
the bull would not pose an insuperable difficulty. It would reduce
converts in an area where the Zarathustrian religion was already
strong just as modern witchcraft, worshipping a horned god, has
obvious difficulties with the Christian churches.

Thus Mithras, the god who changed the heavens, could now
be accepted as the one who sacrificed the bull. But, unlike in the
Ahriman myth, his motive for doing so was to permit the salvation
of us all. It was here that the influence of Hellenistic ideas also
became part of the milieu. The bull, Taurus, was sacrificed, caus-
ing the heavens to change rather than remain permanent. The
blood spilt became the pathway of rebirth and salvation. The sign

at the opposite end of the Milky Way pathway is Scorpio, the scorpion always shown near the testicles of the bull. Thus Taurus and Scorpio take on some of the elements of Cancer and Capricorn, which marked the traditional doorways of incarnation.

The scorpion, incorporated early into the symbolism, became fixed in its representation, always near the genitals. Mithras' right foot consistently holds down the bull's rear hoof for this very reason—to expose the bull's genitals to the scorpion and the scorpion to the view of the initiates. The scorpion does not, however, clutch the genitals of the bull because it wishes to stifle life at its source, as is often stated. Rather it represents the dark and primitive side of ourselves: the nasty self-serving acts we commit or the selfish, angry thoughts we have.

The Mithrasians, from their earliest beginnings, were very insistent on moral behavior from their followers: honesty in business; valor in battle; truthfulness in speech. The scorpion added to these strictures the concept of celibacy or retaining only one wife. The genitals were being contained in their literal sense, since to seek sexual gratification could cause primitive, unworthy thoughts. The image of the scorpion shows the weakness, the underbelly as it were, of our souls. This literal view of the constellation, even outside of the symbolism of astrology, was quite easy to accept. The scorpion was traditionally an animal of Ahriman, and so already associated with evil and unworthy thoughts.

The dog of the icon is generally accepted as Canis Minor, though some suggest Canis Major. In ancient times Canis Minor was often portrayed as leaping, much as it does in the icon. This constellation lies between the Milky Way and the celestial equator, and thus appears to be leaping at the Milky Way itself.

Cumont attributed the dog to Ahura Mazda and interpreted it as a symbol of good, arguing that the dog has always been a highly prized symbol of loyalty. Moreover, the dog recalls one of the two companions of the Iranian Mithra, Shraosha. This companion of the chariot-driving god was loyalty to feudal obligation and represented lawfulness and right action. Such an animal might easily be included in the religious symbolism of a salvationist deity.

The next obvious constellation to include was Hydra the snake, which runs for some distance along the path of the Milky Way. But there were two ways this could be represented. The "head" of Hydra as seen in the sky points from the scorpion toward the bull, and this is how it is often represented in the Tauroctony. But the constellation Taurus actually faces Hydra. If we took it this way, Taurus and Hydra face opposite directions and the snake thus is also shown with its head near the bull's genitals in some Tauroctonies.

Cumont saw the serpent as a symbol of evil, another of Ahriman's creatures. But there is no reason to believe this was the case in the Mithrasian religion, and in fact quite a few reasons to disbelieve it. In scenes of Mithras hunting, the snake is shown as his companion.

That the snake is frequently shown, like the dog, seeking the blood of the bull is itself significant. It seems to indicate the snake is seeking salvation. That it faces the scorpion may indicate it is a primal form of that salvation or that it is open to a choice of seeking salvation.

These were the original figures of the Tauroctony. But over time, the theology of the religion developed. It was no longer the constellations which seemed to be walking that celestial trail, but those on the short side between the Milky Way and the celestial equator taken as a whole.

This development, though, proceeded differently in different areas. One important factor in this differential development was how the Sun-God dealt with this "new" deity. A theological discrepancy developed around the issue of the hierarchy of the various degrees. Thus the inclusion of the next layer of constellations and symbols proved to be far from universal.

What might be called the secondary layer of symbols in the Tauroctony are not treated as consistently as the primary figures. The lion, for instance, appears on a smaller scale than the bull. But it is perfectly in scale with relation to the constellations. The constellation Leo is in fact much shorter than Hydra. It is also slightly smaller than Taurus. That the lion of the icon is in scale with the constellation of the snake is probably deliberate, and therefore significant. After all, Leo is a much larger constellation than Canis Minor, yet the dog, as a primary figure, is shown in scale with the bull. This relative scale seems to indicate that Leo was a later addition to the icon (and never irreplaceable in its scheme of things).[9]

A similar argument can be made for Crater the mixing bowl. This symbol came into the icon at the same time as, and is always associated with, the lion. At times the snake seems more interested in the bowl than the bull. This possibly is because the two constellations are quite close, and in some representations seem to overlap. Likewise Corvus the raven, although possibly an earlier addition to the icon than the lion and the bowl, is shown with some inconsistency, though far less than some other elements. Commonly positioned on the cape of Mithras, he can also perch on the arch of the cave within which Mithras slays the bull. But the raven is never shown flying. Like Corvus the constellation, the raven is always shown with its wings folded. Its role has always been accepted as bearing the message of Sol to Mithras. This message is usually thought to be the order to slay the bull although the raven could simply serve as witness to the act by which Mithras proves his superiority to the Sun-God.

The ray may indicate the Sun in a zodiacal position: a ray, as it were, through Corvus, to Taurus, leading back to another sign. But such a wide range of angles applies that the ray might strike anything from the star Spica the wheat, to Scorpio. We cannot, therefore, determine what theological significance the ray might have played in the religion.

Moreover, Sol traditionally appears paired with Luna. Portrayed in Greek and Roman thought as the sister of Sol, Luna occupies the side of the icon opposite to the Sun-god. Yet Luna plays no discernible part in the religion's mythology. Her placement

---

[9] This does not change the argument that Leo is the adept's degree. That degree could have evolved with somewhat different symbolism vis-a-vis the icon. For example, in the Danubian areas the "lion-headed god" statues don't have the head of a lion but a human head, yet much of the symbolism remains the same.

seems merely to balance the icon in the same way Cautes and Cautopates balance each other. As in most symbolic representations, the figures are subject to the artistic conventions of the times. Some of the elements of the Tauroctony are lost to us, some are only just being revealed, while others may simply express the interpretation of individual artists—much as the beard of Jesus bears no theological significance now, but was merely a sign of lordliness in the Byzantine Empire when beardless representations went out of fashion.

The main thrust of the icon and its meaning and development, however, remain clear. Mithras slays the bull so that we can be saved, as evidenced by the Milky Way and its "path of blood," the constellations that appear in the icon, and the correspondences between the signs of the zodiac and the celestial equator.

These points in the sky showed a path by which the individual might join his god in the permanent communion of the Sacred Meal. In Roman and Syrian areas, the successive stages along this path were marked by the individual's efforts to attain initiation into the various degrees. In the Danube region, this process took on more of the character of an epiphany, the individual undergoing a signal change as he achieved a state of grace.

This geographic distinction in concepts of salvation, part of a wider pattern of differences in the general development of Mithrasism, recalls the central doctrinal issue in the Protestant Reformation—the issue of salvation by faith alone versus salvation by good works. It is interesting that during the Reformation, the battle was fought along much the same front, regions south of the Danube generally remaining Catholic and subscribing to a doctrine of good works, and regions north of the Danube generally espousing the Protestant doctrine of salvation by faith alone. Chapter 5 will focus on the southern form of Mithrasism, which tied redemption to a passage through the degrees of initiation.

Figure 1. Relief of King Antiochus and Mithra, from temple at Commagene in the Taurus Mountains. The Roman Mithras was only one form of a deity worshipped for thousands of years and known in at least six traditions. Recently argument has arisen over how closely we can identify Mithras with the Persian Mithra. But as this relief shows, Mithra (on the right) has much in common with the Mithras. The Phrygian cap, the speckled stars, the Persian trousers, the cape which is often clasped by a serpent, the rays of light from the cap. All these in some form reappear in the Roman mysteries. Though the traditions differ radically, this is the same god who has been worshipped for over 3500 years and continues to be worshipped today. (From Cumont, *Textes et Monuments figures relatifs aux mystères de Mithra*, H. Lamerton, Brussels, 1896, p.188.)

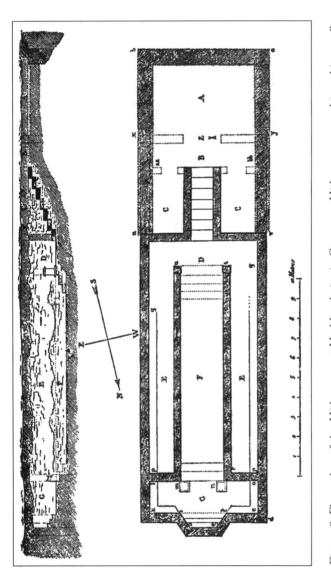

Figure 2. Floor plan of the Mithraeum at Heddernheim in Germany. Mithras was worshipped in small, underground temples. Such a temple, called a Mithraeum, was normally a long aisle with benches on either side. At one end was the entrance, at the other the sacred objects. This gave Mithraea their characteristic long, narrow shape. (From Cumont, *Textes et Monuments figures relatifs aux mystères de Mithra*, H. Lamerton, Brussels, 1896, p. 570.)

Figure 3. Frontal view of the Dura Mithraeum of Dura-Europos. Syria reconstruction at Yale University Art Gallery. Although underground, the temples to Mithras were not dingy. As can be seen here, they had a rich iconography and splendid art. In this scene we view the apse as would a worshipper. An arch distinguishes the apse from the general area of the temple: a series of murals line the walls to a second arch divided into panels and painted with murals. On the floor is the lower altar. All this served to frame the bull-slaying scene (here unfortunately lost), an image which contained many secrets of the religion. (Dura-Europos Collection #68. Copyright © Yale University Art Gallery: used by permission.)

Figure 4. Bull-slaying scene of Mithraeum at S. Maria Capua Verte. This is what a worshipper would have seen as the focus of the Mithraeum and his religion. Fortunately, this mural was merely worn by time, not hacked by Christians with axes. It shows the classic pose of Mithras holding down the bull with one knee, while the other foot is extended to hold down a back leg. One hand pulls back the bull's muzzle, while the other plunges the dagger into its shoulder. On either side of Mithras are miniature versions of himself, torchbearers called Cautes and Cautopates, and around him are other figures common to these scenes: the snake, the dog, the scorpion, Sol and Luna. (From Vermaseren, *Mithraica I: The Mithraeum at S. Maria Capua Verte*, E. J. Brill, Leiden, 1971, Plate III: used by permission.)

Figure 5. Bull-slaying scene and Mithraeum at S. Maria Capua Verte. The bull-slaying scene was the focus of the worshipper's attention, in part, no doubt, because it could be used like a modern masonic tracing board. This view shows the icon as a worshipper would have seen it, and it is easy to see how the Mithraeum's priest could stand before the scene, using it to illustrate various points in his lecture or sermon. (From Vermaseren, *Mithraica I: The Mithraeum at S. Maria Capua Verte*, E. J. Brill, Leiden, 1971, Plate II: used by permission.)

Figure 6. Statue of Mithras slaying the bull. The bull-slaying scene is the most common artifact of the Mithrasian religion. It has been found so often that we can understand what was standard and what was a variation for the sake of emphasis. For example, here the wound of the bull does not spill blood, but three ears of wheat. Clearly, the act of slaying the bull was an act which released fecundity in the world. (Sculpture 1721 ref. XLVIII C, photograph copyright © British Museum, London; used by kind permission.)

Figure 7. Statue of Mithras slaying the bull. In this bull-slaying scene, the wound gushes blood as we would expect. A dog and snake move in to drink the blood. At the same time a scorpion holds the bull's genitals. The scene is many layered: Mithras and the bull are central, while other elements may or may not be included. However, though not represented, they were probably remembered by worshippers. In the same way, the Christian cross does not always have the figure of Jesus on it and almost never includes the crosses of the two thieves, yet worshippers know they belong to the story. (Sculpture 1720 ref. C–800, photograph copyright © British Museum, London; used by permission.)

Figure 8. Mithras the Prophet, left-handed panel of the arch of the
Dura Mithraeum of Dura-Europos, Syria, reconstruction at Yale
University Art Gallery. The Mithrasian religion was a mystery religion, a religion of secrets. In each temple those secrets were
presided over by a priest called a Pater (Father). The Pater was
the highest of a seven-grade initiation system. Here he sits,
enthroned, as he was in life. He wears the Phrygian hat with its
forward-facing topknot, cloak, and Persian tunic and trousers.
(Dura-Europos Collection (Yale 77); photograph copyright © Yale
University Art Gallery; used by permission.)

Figure 9. Mithras the Prophet, right-handed panel of the arch of the Dura Mithraeum of Dura-Europos, Syria, reconstruction at Yale University Art Gallery. Here the Pater sits enthroned. The scroll in his left hand and other, epigraphic evidence, proves the Mithrasian was a liturgical religion, though the sacred writings are now lost to us. Any argument that there were no sacred writings is wrong. Note the staff in his right hand: this and the Phrygian cap are badges of his rank. The sword with a hook and the ring are not evident, but if the ring was worn on the right hand it would not be visible here. (Dura-Europos Collection (Yale 78); photograph copyright © Yale University Art Gallery; used by permission.)

Figure 10. Mural of initiation at S. Maria Capua Verte. In this badly damaged mural we see the candidate, naked, on one knee, and apparently
blindfolded like a Mason. His hands are behind him, and from the
Christian polemic we know they were bound by chicken guts. Behind the
candidate, almost lost, is a standing figure. This second figure's hands
are outstretched near the candidate's head in some kind of blessing:
healing, imbuing with magical energy ("narbarze"), or laying on of hands
in apostolic succession. (From Vermaseren, *Mithraica I: The Mithraeum
at S. Maria Capua Verte*, E. J. Brill, Leiden, 1971, Plate XXV; used by permission.)

Figure 11. Mural of initiation at S. Maria Capua Verte. This initiation may involve the "Miles" or "Soldier" degree, but the painting is so damaged the figure on the left may be a Pater. The candidate is naked, blindfolded, and on one knee. Behind him is a standing figure, perhaps carrying a sword. Before the candidate is a Miles or a Pater. He may wear the centurion's helmet or Pater's Phrygian cap, carry the kitbag or have a billowing cape, and hold a spear or sword, which are badges of the two degrees. The difficulty interpreting this scene helps remind us of the gaps in our knowledge of this religion. (From Vermaseren, *Mithraica I: The Mithraeum at S. Maria Capua Verte*, E. J. Brill, Leiden, 1971, Plate XXII; used by permission.)

Figure 12. Mural of initiation at S. Maria Capua Verte. The candidate for initiation is naked, on both knees, and perhaps no longer blindfolded. His hands are across his chest in what would now be called the Osiris position. His hands are held in place by the man behind him. Next to the candidate is what appears to be a loaf of bread. Standing in front of the candidate is another figure so damaged that we cannot identify him. (From Vermaseren, *Mithraica I: The Mithraeum at S. Maria Capua Verte*, E. J. Brill, Leiden, 1971, Plate XXVIII; used by permission.)

Figure 13. Zodiac of Daressy. Astrology was central to the secrets of the religion of Mithras, so it is not surprising to find astrological themes common. Here the zodiac is split into three concentric circles, perhaps intimating increasingly more potent inner secrets. (Photograph from Fr. Boll, *Sphaera*, Leipzig, 1903, Plate IV, in Vermaseren, *Mithraica II: The Mithraeum at Ponza*, E. J. Brill, Leiden, 1974, Plate XXV; used by permission.)

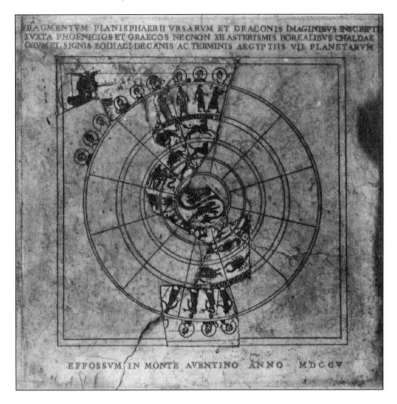

Figure 14. Planisphere. Tabula Bianchini. This planisphere shows how integral astrology was to the Mithrasian religion. The concentric circles may have formed a kind of visual table of correspondences, showing what the various constellations meant in the context of the religion. (Paris, Louvre, original plate courtesy of Prof. Noel Duval; photograph: Chuzeville, in Vermaseren, *Mithraica II: The Mithraeum at Ponza,* E. J. Brill, Leiden, 1974, Plate XXVI; used by permission.)

Figure 15 (opposite). Detail of planisphere. Tabula Bianchini. This close-up of the planisphere shows the center was a snake entwined around two bears. The snake is probably the constellation Hydra and the snake from the bull-slaying scene. The bears are Ursa Major and Ursa Minor (the Big and Little Dippers). In Roman times Ursa Major contained the

pole star, so it never set. It was sometimes referred to as a bull, and as such seems to have entered Mithrasian theology. (Original plate courtesy of Prof. Noel Duval; photograph: Chuzeville, in Vermaseren, *Mithraica II: The Mithraeum at Ponza*, E. J. Brill, Leiden, 1974, Plate XXVII; used by permission.)

Figure 16. Relief of Mithras slaying the bull, flanked on either side by Cautes and Cautopates, within a zodiac circle. The importance of astrology to the religion can be seen in this relief. Mithras' slaying of the bull was a cosmic event. Here the scene is placed within a zodiac. The four main figures—Cautes, Mithras, Cautopates, and the bull—probably represent the spring equinox, summer solstice, autumn equinox, and winter solstice, respectively. In another sense, by slaying the bull, Mithras created the precession of equinoxes, an astronomical phenomenon which had just been discovered at the time of the founding of the religion. (Original plate courtesy of Prof. Dr. D. W. Grimes in Vermaseren, *Mithraica II: The Mithraeum at Ponza*, E. J. Brill, Leiden, 1974, Plate XXXIII; used by permission.)

Figure 17. Bull-slaying scene, relief from the Esquiline in Rome. Once a candidate became a member, the religion was revealed in stages or degrees. Though he might look at the bull-slaying scene, it's hard to believe the new member understood all of its import at once—the symbolism was too rich. This bull-slaying scene includes the arch in a cave. Mithrasians thought of the universe as a cave with stars studding the walls. The seven stars here are both the seven planets and the seven degrees of the religion. (Musei Vaticani, Neg. no. XXI.15.35. Original plate courtesy Prof. Dr. Carlo Pietrangeli; photograph: Archivo Fotografico Gall, in Vermaseren, *Mithraica III: The Mithraeum at Marino,* E. J. Brill, Leiden, 1982, Plate XXII; used by permission.)

Figure 18. Fire shovel, Odessa. This object was identified incorrectly in the Dutch text as a bronze perfume-burner. The secrets of the Mithrasian religion were doled out through a degree system. But for any such group this means at some point the member ceased to learn and was said to have learned: he became a full member of the group. This degree, the "adept's degree," was the Leo (Lion). The symbols of the Leo were the thunderbolt, the sistrum (rattle) and the fire shovel (fire was the element of the degree). A fine example of a fire shovel is shown here. At its center is Sol,

Figure 19. Lion-headed statue currently in the Vatican Museum. Second only to the bull-slaying scene in frequency are the so-called "Lion-headed god" statues. In fact they are a representation or ide-alization of the degree of Leo (Lion), showing the various attributes of the degree. Note the thunderbolt over the heart of this statue. The thunderbolt was one of the badges of the degree and here seems to indicate the psychic cen-ter of the heart has been opened. He holds the keys to the heavens (later adopted as the Papal symbol), a staff of authority, and is entwined by a snake. The wings are marked with the symbols of the four seasons, placing the lion-headed statues with the bull-slaying scene as a solar symbol. (From Cumont, *Textes et Monuments figures relatifs aux mystères de Mithra*, H. Lamerton, Brussels, 1896, p. 238.)

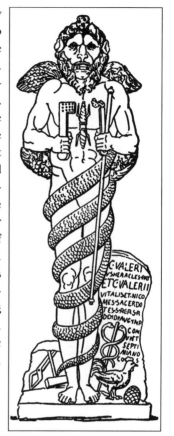

(Figure 18 cont.) the Sun-god, who played a very important part in the mythology of the religion. He is surrounded by the zodiac. The handle is a sheaf of wheat, recalling the wound of the bull which sometimes spills wheat, and its tail, which sometimes turns into wheat. Finally, the handle ends in an eagle's head, the eagle being the bird of Jupiter, and Jupiter being the planet of this degree. (Archaeological Museum. Original plate from E. de Belin de Bellu; *Olbia*, E. J. Brill, Leiden, 1971, Plate LXXVII, 2, reproduced in Vermaseren, *Mithraica II: The Mithraeum at Ponza*, E. J. Brill, Leiden, 1974, Plate XXIV; used by permission.)

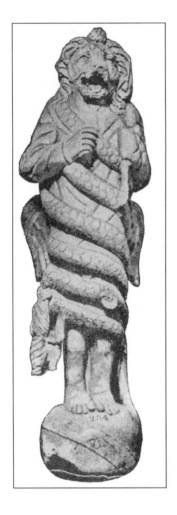

Figure 20. Lion-headed statue from Florence. This lion-headed statue stands on a globe with two bands (one of which is quite worn). One band is the zodiac, the other is the celestial equator, the line of constellations touched by a "band" created by projecting the Earth's equator out to the stars. That the zodiac should be there is not surprising; that the celestial equator is there opens doors to deeper Mithrasian symbolism. (From Cumont, *Textes et Monuments figures relatifs aux mystères de Mithra*, H. Lamerton, Brussels, 1896, p. 259.)

Figure 21. Sketch of a lion-headed statue found in Rome in the 16th century.
Here the snake entwines the lion-headed
statue three times. The snake can coil
the figure anywhere from three to seven
times. Perhaps this is because the constellation Hydra, depending on how you
count, can be said to have between three
and seven undulations. Similar discrep-
ancies occur in the number of undulations of the snake in the bull-slaying
scene. However, the snake always has
its head on the head of the lion-headed
figure, which must mean the head, like
the heart, was seen by Mithrasians as a
center of power. This is the only case of
the snake seeming to enter the lion's
mouth, and since the original statue is
now lost we may question the veracity
of this detail. (Drawing from Cumont,
*Textes et Monuments figures relatifs aux
mystères de Mithra*, H. Lamerton,
Brussels, 1896, p. 196.)

Figure 22. Lion-headed figure on relief in white marble found in Mithraeum in Rome in the 16th century. Franz Cumont describes the snake as becoming four snakes and entwining the wings rather than the body. It seems rather to be the one snake which has been sundered, with the Leo's power fully unleashed. That is why the breath of the figure reaches the fire. It holds two torches, one in either hand. Fire, of course, was the element of the Leo degree. (From Cumont, *Textes et Monuments figures relatifs aux mystères de Mithra,* H. Lamerton, Brussels, 1896, p. 196.)

Figure 23. Mithras born from stone, relief from the crypt of St. Clements at Rome. Apart from slaying the bull, Mithras was notable for other wonders. This relief shows his miraculous birth from a stone. In one hand he holds the dagger with which he will one day slay the bull; in the other he holds a torch with which he shall illuminate the world. (From Cumont, *Textes et Monuments figures relatifs aux mystères de Mithra,* H. Lamerton, Brussels, 1896, p. 202.)

Figure 24 (pages 100 & 101). Mural of Mithras slaying the bull, with side panels, from Barberini Mithraeum. In many cases the bull-slaying scene was not only symbolically rich, but was accompanied by side panels with further scenes of theological importance. This one is badly faded but still shows some surprising images. The panel on the left, second from the top, for example, shows Saturn bearing a compass. On the right, second from the top, is Mithras riding the chariot to the heavens after his mission on earth. Below that Mithras and Sol stand on either side of an altar to complete a treaty. Below that Mithras seems to invoke a rainbow and cause plants to grow; he has one hand pointing up and another pointing down rather like the tarot card called "The World." At the bottom, Mithras puts a hand on the forehead of Sol or a candidate for initiation, a blessing he reinforces by showing what appears to be a joint of meat, a reminder of the Sacred Meal. Note that the main panel is framed by an arch of zodiacal signs, in the middle of which is a human figure entwined by a snake. The head is missing, but it seems to be a lion-headed figure such as we've seen before. (Original photograph, Antonio Solazzi, Rome, in Vermaseren, *Mithraica III: The Mithraeum at Marino,* E. J. Brill, Leiden, 1982, Plate XIV and XV; used by permission.)

Figure 24.

Figure 25. Mithras slays the bull. On each side of this bull-slaying scene are three small panels. On the right, from top down, we have Mithras on a horse, probably hunting though the left arm (carrying a bow?) is now missing. Next, Sol kneels before Mithras, an altar between the two. Sol holds a dagger, Mithras what looks like a taper. The lowest right hand panel is again Sol kneeling before Mithras to receive a blessing of one hand on the head and the other holding a joint of meat. On the left side at the bottom we have another birth of Mithras, this time witnessed by Cautes and Cautopates. Above that, perhaps part of the same scene, Saturn reclines, either musing or witnessing Mithras' birth. The top panel is indistinct, and could be a gigantomachy. (Relief from Nersae, Rome, National Museum. Original plate courtesy of Prof. Dr. Elisa Lissi-Caronna; photograph: Caldarazzo, in Vermaseren, *Mithraica III: The Mithraeum at Marino*, E. J. Brill, Leiden, 1982, Plate XX; used by permission.)

Figure 26 (opposite). Relief of bull-slaying scene, with side and top panels. This bull-slaying scene has three sets of panels at the left, right and top, each of which seems to follow a set theme. The four panels on the right show Mithras struggling with the bull prior to slaying it. At the top the bull grazes peacefully. Mithras seizes it and carries it away on his shoulders (second panel). In the third panel the bull breaks free and runs with Mithras hanging onto its neck. In the final panel, Mithras has recap-

tured the bull and drags it by its hind legs, while the bull's muzzle drags along the ground.

The left-side panels start at the top with Mithras being born from stone, holding a dagger in one hand and the globe of world dominion in the other. Below this, Jupiter and Saturn conclude an agreement for the passing on of power, symbolized by the handing over of the thunderbolt. This third panel is Saturn reclining, musing, holding a knife. The final panel shows Mithras normally described as holding the Earth, but the device is more like a ring, such as a zodiac. If these panels should be read as a story, Mithras has taken over the rulership of the universe from Jupiter.

The top pattern is most interesting. On both outermost panels Mithras tends a tree while one of the seasonal winds (the giant head) gusts behind him. The next panel inward in both cases shows the miracle of the rock, when Mithras fired an arrow into a rock and caused it to gush forth a spring (alternatively shot an arrow into a cloud to make it rain). Of the two central panels, the one on the left shows Mithras riding the chariot into the sky, the chariot being driven by Sol. On the right Sol drives an earth-bound chariot, and perhaps even a plough. This set of panels seems to describe Mithras' role on Earth, prior to going to the heavens. (From Neuenheim, Karlsruhe, Badishes Landesmuseum. Original plate courtesy Dr. Bernhard Cammerer, in Vermaseren, *Mithraica III: The Mithraeum at Marino*, E. J Brill, Leiden, 1982, Plate XXI; used by permission.)

Figure 27. Altar of Cresces (Marino). This altar is similar to the double cube altar still used by magicians today, save that it has capitals top and bottom. It stood at the back, just before the bull-slaying scene. On either side it shows the treaty between Mithras and Sol. On the front is an inscription: INVICTO DEO CRESCES ACTOR ALFI SEBERI D(onum) P(osuit). Mithras is often addressed as "Invicto Deo" ("Invincible God") or some variant of that name. He is often, for example, called "Mithras Sol Invictus," or "Mithras the Invincible Sun-God." Inscriptions such as this and graffiti are the only textual evidence we have for the religion. (Original plate by Antonio Solazzi, Rome, in Vermaseren, *Mithraica III: The Mithraeum at Marino,* E. J. Brill, Leiden, 1982, Plate II; used by permission.

Figure 28. Altar found at Sarmizegetusa. This altar bears an inscription containing the mysterious word "nabarze." This has been interpereted to mean "victorious," making the inscription to "the victorious god," but the Latin term "Invictus" ("Invincible") was already in common use. The term "nabarze" may mean "magical power," rather like prana or elan vital. Such a term did not exist in Latin form, making its use here more logical. (From Cumont, *Textes et Monuments figures relatifs aux mystères de Mithra,* H. Lamerton, Brussels, 1896, p. 281.)

NABARZE
DEO
PROSALAMPLIATI
AVG·N·DISPET
SVA·SVORVMQ
OMNIVM
PROTASVIKAR
EIVS

Figure 29. Relief of Sol, the Sun-God. It should be remembered that the religion of Mithras did not focus solely on the god, himself. Other deities were involved, as with Sol, the god of the sun, shown here and earlier in figures 4, 18, 24, 25, 26 and 27. These other entities were vital in and of themselves, if in supporting roles. These beings, too, received their share of adoration. (From Cumont, *Textes et Monuments figures relatifs aux mystères de Mithra,* H. Lamerton, Brussels, 1896, p. 202.)

Figure 30. Reliefs of Cautes and Cautopates, the torchbearers of Mithras. Highly important to the Mithrasian religion are Cautes and Cautopates, who represent morning and evening, spring and autumn, spring equinox and autumn equinox, respectively. The origin of their names is unknown, but they formed a significant element in the symbolism of the religion. (The Louvre, Paris, in Vermaseren, *Mithraica IV: Le Monument D'Ottaviano Zeno et le Culte de Mithra Sur le Celius*, E. J. Brill, Leiden, 1978, Plate XVIII; used by permission.)

Figure 31. Gem in the Archaeological Museum, Florence. The images of Mithras are found in murals, reliefs, statues, and, as here, on gems as talismans. But gems show their talismanic nature by showing symbols in an assortment chosen for power rather than theme. The symbols are still Mithrasian, but taken out of context. In this bullslaying scene, the upper region is filled with a caduceus, a thunderbolt, a raven, an unhooked sword, a star, and other objects. These are all references to the various degrees of the religion. (From *Corpus Inscriptorum et Monumentum Religionis Mithriacae,* Vol. II, Martinus Nijhoff, Norwell, MA, 1956-1960, No. 2354, in Vermaseren, *Mithraica IV: Le Monument D'Ottaviano Zeno et le Culte de Mithra Sur le Celius,* E. J. Brill, Leiden, 1978, Plate XXX, 1; used by permission.)

Figure 32. Gem in the Archaeological Museum, Udine. This gem shows the bull-slaying scene with Cautes and Cautopates on either side of Mithras. Beneath the bull are the scorpion and the dog, as well as a fish in place of the snake. In the upper portion we have busts of Sol and Luna on the left and right, respectively. To the left of Cautes is a small tree holding an object which might be a bull's head. There are six small and one particularly large star (the last could be a flower, but has no stem). There are also several degree badges in a sword, a thunderbolt, a caduceus, and a raven. As with other gems, the themes of Mithras remain consistent, but the magical use seems to dictate employing as many themes as possible, encompassing as many degrees, images, currents if you will, as possible. (Original plate from *Corpus Inscriptorum et Monumentum Religionis Mithriacae*, Vol. II, Martinus Nijhoff, Norwell, MA, 1956-1960, No. 2355, in Vermaseren, *Mithraica IV: Le Monument D'Ottaviano Zeno et le Culte de Mithra Sur le Celius*, E. J. Brill, Leiden, 1978, Plate XXX, 2; used by permission.)

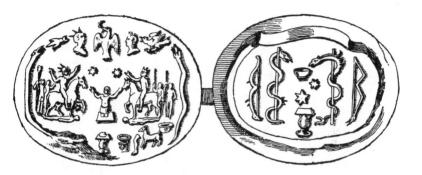

Figure 33. Mithrasian gem. In this case we have Mithras being born from the stone, on either side a horsed figure, each with two staff-bearing attendants. The horsed figures are probably Cautes and Cautopates, who we know attended the birth. The other figures are probably shepherds, who also witnessed the miracle. Around are common symbols of the Mithrasian religion: Sol and Luna busts, serpents, a dog, a mixing bowl, a raven. At the bottom is the cup and bread for the communion Mithras is destined to institute. (From Cumont, *The Mysteries of Mithra*, 2nd revised edition, translation from the French by Thomas J. McCormack, Dover Publications, New York, 1903, figure 28, p. 124.)

Figure 34. Mithras in triumph. This unusual relief shows Mithras apparently after the bull-slaying, reinforcing the cosmic importance of that event. Mithras stands on the bull, one foot on the animal's head, the other on its back. In one hand he holds a dagger and in the other the globe of world domination: the very objects he holds in some scenes of his birth from stone. At the top on the left is the bust of Sol, at the right a bust of Luna. Several figures from the bull-slaying are visible: at the bottom are the dog and the snake; by Mithras' legs are Cautes and Cautopates, above Cautes is the raven. By Mithras' knee, but not near the bull's genitals, is the scorpion. This change in position must carry

Figure 35. Mithrasian communion, fragment found at Konjica, Bosnia. The religion of Mithras included a communion of water miraculously transformed to wine and small loaves or wafers of bread marked with a cross. The tripod in front of the table, here, shows the bread. Sitting at the table are Mithras and Sol, or, perhaps, their representatives in a Pater and a Heliodromus. On the left are a Perses (Persian: inner figure) and a Corax (Raven). On the right is a Miles (Soldier: inner figure) and a Leo (Lion). Thus six of the seven degrees of the religion are represented here, with only the Nymphus (Bride) missing. Note the small lion next to the tripod: this serves as a reminder that only with the degree of Leo was a member a full participant in the Sacred Meal. (From Cumont, *Textes et Monuments figures relatifs aux mystères de Mithra*, H. Lamerton, Brussels, 1896, p.175.)

(Figure 34 cont.) a theological meaning but we don't understand what it is. This relief, as a whole, is a unique bridge between Mithras' great act and its aftermath. (Relief in possession of the Altieri family, in Vermaseren, *Mithraica IV: Le Monument D'Ottaviano Zeno et le Culte de Mithra Sur le Celius*, E. J. Brill, Leiden, 1978, Plate IX; used by permission.)

Chapter Five

The Degrees
of Initiation

The Mithrasian religion encompassed seven grades: Corax (Raven), Nymphus (Bride), Miles (Soldier), Leo (Lion), Perses (Persian), Heliodromus (Messenger of the Sun or Sun-Runner), and Pater (Father). Various inscriptions and Christian polemic have shown this hierarchy to be consistent throughout at least the southern half of the Empire, but our best evidence for the order appears in a mosaic in the Mithraeum at Ostia.

Here the floor was set in the pattern of a ladder. Between the rungs are the name and devices of each grade. This is the only place where we not only have the degrees but their whole order. But even here there have been certain assumptions made about the degrees that just are not warranted.

The animal degrees of Corax and Leo have been passed off, for example, as the remnants of the widespread primitive practice of imitating animals. People in these degrees are described wearing masks like ravens' and lions' heads, respectively. But the wearing of religious or theatrical masks was not uncommon in the Roman Empire. The priests of Anubis, the Egyptian god of death, were known to wear masks shaped like the heads of jackals. Moreover, there is no evidence that members ever wore the attributes or mask associated with the degrees in reliefs—at least not as a common practice. And while it is possible that such masks were generally made of perishable materials like wood or cloth, it seems unlikely that none would have been made of more durable materials like clay or metal, materials in common use elsewhere.

Table 2. The Attributes of the Mithrasian Degrees.

Degree	Translation	Planet	Attributes
Corax	Raven	Mercury	Raven, Caduceus, Cup
Nymphus	Bride	Venus	Veil, Lamp, Mirror*
Miles	Soldier	Mars	Lance, Helmet, Kitbag
Leo	Lion	Jupiter	Fire shovel, Sistrum, Thunderbolt
Perses	Persian	Moon	Crescent Moon & Star, Sickle, Hooked Sword
Heliodromus	Sun-Messenger	Sun	Torch, Whip, Nimbus
Pater	Father	Saturn	Staff & Ring, Persian Cap, Curved Sword

* I should point out the ladder mosaic at Ostia is damaged, and the third item of the Nymphus is lost. However, a mural in Ostia shows Aphrodite with a veil, lamp, and mirror, and this no doubt was meant to refer to the degree. Some variation did exist, however. Sometimes the veil of the Nymphus is a diadem, sometimes the mirror is a torch. But these are minor differences: Many brides in Rome wore diadem and veil, and undoubtedly one referred to the other; likewise, a torch creates and a mirror reflects light.

The masks shown in various Mithraic art works may be merely representational, meant to show the grade of the individual and the duties of that grade. Similar conventions were used in early Imperial art. For example, the Emperor was often painted with a halo, a convention later used for Christian saints. No one suggests the Emperors of Rome wore gold plates or that their heads glowed. The same explanation may apply to the Ravens and Leos of Mithrasian religion.

Questions have also been raised concerning the degree of Nymphus or Bride. Why would a group that excluded women have such a markedly feminine degree?

The possibility of any homosexual element can be discounted for the simplest of reasons: the Christian polemicists never mentioned it. Had they any opportunity to suggest sexual activity of any sort, they would have done so. After all, *orgia*, from which we derive our word orgy, originally meant any pagan festival held at night; even those in which the members had already been castrated. That the Christians did not impute any sexual motive to the Mithrasians in any form—let alone the obvious chance to attack with a charge of homosexuality—indicates that sexuality never played a significant role in the religion except for the celibacy mentioned before.

Why, then, a grade called the Bride? It would seem to indicate that the Mithrasian degrees were not haphazardly designed, or remnants of earlier practices, or simple holdovers from some previous system of degrees taken over by the Mithrasians.

Instead we are looking at a tightly organized system of correspondences, in which each degree was associated with certain virtues, certain principles, certain badges of office, a planet, and a part of the central icon which was the core of the religion. A closer look at this system will help explain the degrees of Mithrasian initiation. Table 2 gives a chart of the attributes of the Mithrasian degrees.

An occultist will immediately note that these attributes have common aspects. Nearly every degree has something that can be carried; nearly every degree has something that can be worn. The Corax can carry the caduceus and wear (at least in reliefs and murals) a raven's head; the Nymphus can wear the veil and carry the mirror; the Miles can carry the lance and wear the helmet. To an occultist, this makes sense because it fits the expected pattern of an initiation series: change in the soul of the initiate.

Moreover, in all religions, the spiritual principle is taught through a compound of spirituality and another virtue. In the case of Christianity, it was compassion; in the case of Mithrasism it was valor. Thus each degree was linked through its attributes to a symbol of "duty" (see Table 3). Together, these attributes and duties provide a reasonably clear picture of the spiritual teaching of each degree.

One point of interest which emerges from the Tables is the symbolic importance of the head. Four of the degrees have a symbol worn on the head. Corax could be symbolized by a person with a raven's head, as could a Leo by a person with a lion's head. Moreover, the Leo was associated with the lion-headed statues. The Perses has a badge of the crescent Moon in a triangle, but in a relief from Konjica, Bosnia showing a Sacred Meal, he wears a Phrygian cap distinguished from the Pater's by his badge. Furthermore, each of the three degrees that doesn't have a symbol which can be worn on the head has a symbol linked to the head. Clearly

Table 3. The Duties of the Mithrasian Degrees.

Degree	Carried/Active	Worn	Duty
Corax	Caduceus	Raven('s head)	Cup
Nymphus	Mirror	Veil	Lamp
Miles	Lance	Helmet	Kitbag
Leo	Fire shovel	Thunderbolt	Sistrum
Perses	Sword	Moon & Star	Sickle
Heliodromus	Torch	Nimbus	Whip
Pater	Sword	Persian Cap	Staff/Ring

this indicates the symbolic significance of how the members of each degree thought.

Likewise, the items carried symbolized the individual's duty, which was linked to the moral component of the degree. The Corax, for instance, carries a cup, symbol of humility, to indicate their role as a servitor at the Sacred Meal in which they did not participate. By contrast, the Pater's staff and ring symbolized authority or infinity. Each degree carried some symbol of its obligation to the world.

The third category of symbol common to all the degrees was an elongated object. These items are alike in that each of them is a long object carried at one end, normally by a handle. The symbols themselves seem to indicate the secret the degree will teach the member.

Corax

Following a spectacular initiation we will discuss in chapter 6, the prospective member became a Corax, meaning "raven." The degree corresponded to the planet Mercury; its three devices were the cup, the caduceus, and the raven. The constellation with which it was associated was Corvus; the raven in the Tauroctony became its icon. The moral it taught was humility. That the degree related to the planet Mercury we know from several sources, including the mosaic at Ostia and the inscription at St. Prisca, which reads "Nama Coracibus tutela Mercurii" or "Holy Raven of Mercury's tutelage."[1]

The main task of the Coraxes was to serve the higher degrees during the Sacred Meal. They brought the food on plates and laid it before the Leos. They took away remnants and put these in the burial pits often found near Mithraea. They may also have performed "charwoman" and "batman" duties, cleaning the Mithraeum and

---

[1] Quoted in M. J. Vermaseren, *Mithras: The Secret God* (London: Chatto and Windus, 1959) p. 141. This inscription may have been a formula as well as a description.

seeing to the dressing of various participants in their ceremonial regalia. They may have shared these and cooking duties with the Nymphuses and possibly even the wives of the regular members.

All this was designed to instill a sense of humility in the Corax, in keeping with the Mithrasians' self-portrayal as an elite. Closed societies, particularly those in a minority position, must have some element or promise which elevates them above the general community. Without that element of superiority, there would be no reason to join or remain in the group. Even claims of equality are insufficient; the minority group must claim superiority.

The inevitable mystique of superiority is enhanced by forcing members of the lower grades to work for members of higher grades, or for newer members to work for members of longer standing. It also seems to be essential that the superiority of higher members be described as an additional burden rather than a privilege. Without this there would be no higher purpose to getting the newer or lesser members to undertake tasks for their betters; it would be mere indentured servitude.

For example, prospective members of the Knights Templar were reminded of the great hardship membership would inevitably bring. Members of the Golden Dawn seeking membership of the inner order were advised that all their previous achievements of membership would now be laid aside. In both cases, a culture of lesser members serving higher members predominated. It was, in fact, a culture of patronage.

The Corax represented the first stage of this belief of a special role. The Coraxes had to serve those higher up; they had to change the way they were in order to progress. The symbolism of the grade confirms this. Mercury was the messenger of the gods, and Corvus was the messenger of the Tauroctony—it was the raven who brought Mithras the message of the Sun-god. But Mercury was also the psychopomp. That is, he was the guide of the souls of the dead, taking them from their bodies to the River Styx where Charon the boatman would ferry them to Hades. This tells us that the message the raven brought to Mithras concerned the death of the bull.

The raven was also a scavenger, a harbinger of doom. He had a low reputation in the ancient world. Little wonder he became the servant of others. As in the image of Sol and Mithras shaking hands over an altar of oath where the raven is shown pecking at the meat, the Coraxes probably fed themselves as they went. The Leos may have participated in the ritual meal but no doubt everyone consumed the food.

The image of the raven also symbolized the thoughts of the first degree members—scavengers of ideas, as it were. Like a bird flying from place to place, the Corax's thoughts were likely to go from one thing to another, reinforcing the notion that Mithrasism emerged from an occult milieu such that they not only added material they also organized much of what had existed prior to their formation.

The morals of the Coraxes, too, were those of the scavenger. Raven's were seen as repositories of vice, as the fables of Aesop will attest. The three devices of office represent this bias. The cup is not a mixing bowl, but a single-handled drinking cup, reminding the Corax of his duty to serve the members of higher degrees at the Sacred Meal. It is possible that each Corax was sponsored by or otherwise assigned to an individual Leo, acting in a sense as his batman. The Corax would be responsible for helping dress his Leo in any ceremonial regalia. He would run normal errands, and otherwise act like a newly inducted soldier is normally treated by those who had been soldiers longer—like a slave. Thus the Corax learned the virtue of humility.

The raven or raven's head reminded the Corax of the reason for this treatment. His state was lowly. He was prey to immoral thoughts and activities. He was touched by death and not yet wholly redeemed. Like the alchemical symbol of the raven's head, the Corax represented the raw material, the original ore which had to be refined to be of use. The Corax had to be trained to control his thoughts and to understand death.

Thought control seems to have been vital to the Mithrasians, as shown by each degree having some symbol pertaining to the head. Some have suggested that the different head gear merely provided a convenient way of spotting different degrees in a crowd. But the Mithrasians, almost uniquely in the Empire, had no public procession. Since these devices had no value in separating individual ranks in a crowd, the interest in the head must have had esoteric import.

The third device of the Corax is the caduceus, a staff with two snakes twined around it, representing Mercury's role as the guide of the dead. Reincarnation was an integral part of the Mithrasian religion, as shown by the astrological symbolism of the Milky Way as the ladder of souls. Reincarnation was an accepted belief in Roman society generally, and was a strong, though not dominant, stream of thought in the Zarathustrian religion. The Corax was guided symbolically through the processes normally reserved for the dead. He was drossed, to borrow an alchemical or metallurgical term—the impurities were removed from his thoughts and from his soul in order that he might return to the source of things. Only when the dross had been removed could he go on to the next stage of Nymphus.

Nymphus

The second Mithrasic degree was Nymphus, called the Bride. Although the planet of this degree, Venus, seems to require a feminine imagery, Perses, assigned to the Moon, has no parallel feminine image. The seeming incongruity of this female imagery in a religion which excluded women has been discussed. Suffice it here to note the planetary and stellar references which drove that imagery. The devices of the degree were the bridal veil or diadem, the mirror or torch, and the lamp. The constellation of the degree was probably Spica, the wheat ear, held by Virgo. This constellation and perhaps its planet, Venus, is what made the feminine images of the degree necessary.

The feminine imagery deriving from the astrological attributes of the degree, also ties in with an interest the Mithrasians had in the myth of Cupid and Psyche, a story particularly popular in the second century C.E. Reliefs of the couple have been found in Mithraea. As we can see from Lucius Apuleius' work, *The Golden Ass,* the myth was considered an initiatory story, an interpretation which fits well with the symbolism of the Nymphus degree. Taken as an allegory of the discovery of the soul of a man (and used as such in *The Golden Ass)*, the myth recounts a story of self-discovery and introspection. All the devices of the Nymphus degree have a similar theme.

The diadem and veil relate to the veiling of the bride, a custom continued even today. It is significant that the word "nymphus" means not only bride, but secret. The task of the Nymphus was thus to uncover internal secrets.

The Nymphus sought the internal world, the world normally hidden behind a veil. The Nymphus carries a lamp, to assist in its task of illuminating or shedding light on the inner world. In this context, the image of Venus, the third brightest object in the heavens after the Sun and the Moon, is most appropriate.

The Nymphus also carries a mirror, the symbol of self-examination—of looking into one's internal self. In other words, by the light of teachings (the lamp), the Nymphus would look into himself (the mirror), and see himself as he really was rather than how he wished to be seen (the veil). In this process of self-discovery, the major virtue attributed to brides was emphasized: patience in the pursuit of self-understanding.

In this context, the Nymphus learned Mithrasian theology and the responses required by ritual. Indeed, the Nymphuses seemed to have formed a kind of sacred chorus, at least at Dura-Europas where as many as sixteen are portrayed in a single relief—the only case of multiple members of any degree other than Corax and Leo.

A surviving text by Firmicus Maternus can be interpreted as indicating such a chorus. Unfortunately the key word of the text is disputed—the Greek text could read either "aide" or "ide," translating respectively as "sing" or "behold." If the correct translation is "sing," then the text reads "Sing, Nymphus, hail Nymphus, hail new light."[2] I think this interpretation is correct because the mean-

---

[2] Quoted in Vermaseren, *Mithras*, p. 143. Also appears in Franz Cumont, "The Dura Mithraeum" *Mithraic Studies*, trans. and ed. John R. Hinnells (Manchester: Manchester University Press, 1975), pp. 200-201.

ing seems to be not the Nymphus being hailed, but the Nymphus doing the hailing of the new light. This new light included the light of knowledge. At this stage, the inner secrets of the Mithrasian community almost certainly were not revealed. By parallel with the Golden Dawn, in the early degrees, the student was given nothing that could not have been found in books commonly available. What differed was that these various elements were drawn together in an entirely new way, giving them a coherence and unity they had previously lacked. Investiture with the various devices of the degrees doubtless provided great opportunity to impart to the initiate knowledge of their relevance to Mithrasian doctrine. The Golden Dawn and the Freemasons both use investiture in initiation in this manner.

Miles

Miles means "Soldier." Not a surprising degree given the recruitment of so many soldiers in the religion. Nor is it surprising that the degree was attributed to the planet Mars, and employed for its symbols a soldier's kitbag, a lance, and a helmet.

These martial symbols tell us a great deal about the degree of Miles. The devices portrayed at Ostia, for instance, would apply to a rank no higher than centurion (a commander's helmet had its comb sideways to distinguish him from his troops). In other words the Miles was an ordinary soldier, not an officer. The dedications we have, however, are largely from officers of some rank—Commanders-in-Chief, commandants of whole legions, are not infrequent. We have governors and Praetors. These men helped run an empire and yet found satisfaction in a degree which took as its model the lowly foot soldier.

Mithra, the Iranian version of the deity, was a god of battle. He granted victory over the armies of the Lie, both the physical and metaphysical forms of the concept. Mithras was a god of salvation. As such, all his followers might be considered as soldiers engaged in a battle against evil. They, too, faced physical enemies motivated by evil and the temptation of evil, But the Miles was something different.

Tertullian[3] gives a brief description of the initiation into the degree. A candidate was offered a wreath on a sword. Such wreaths or garlands were symbols of courage and a reward for meritorious service. The candidate, however, had to push away the wreath which had been laid upon his brow, saying that Mithras alone was his wreath.

The candidate was also marked on the forehead. The order is not described in Tertullian, but I believe the mark came second and was made with ash or clay. The mark was probably the same mark of the cross that Mithrasians used on the bread they ate as the flesh of their savior. The refusal to accept honors, the marking as if a slave, and the image of a common soldier rather than an officer all imply the virtue that most infused this degree must have been sacrifice.

The duty of the degree is represented by the kitbag. In this a soldier carried his belongings, rations of food, and items for setting up camp each night. Men were given the tent, some stakes, and a shovel or other equipment which together made them an operating unit in the job of setting up the nightly camp. The kitbag symbolized the dedication of the soldier and the willingness to go anywhere, do anything, follow any order. Even if they were moved from one of the quiet provinces to a frontier, soldiers accepted their lot and were expected, then more than now, to be ready to lay down their lives in the line of duty. Soldiers in the Empire were moved quite often. Some individual soldiers served in what is now Morocco, Egypt, Syria, and the English-Scottish border. Their lives were in every way in the hands of the Empire.

The lance represented the active side of the degree; the strength and fortitude required of any soldier; the means by which the soldier comes to the sense of sacrifice he must hold.

---

[3] Tertullian, *De Corona*, quoted in Vermaseren, *Mithras*, p. 145.

It seems certain that members of the Miles degree were sworn to be or were inculcated to be bulwarks for the religion. They were reminded their debt was to the god who offered them salvation.

They were no doubt reminded of the role of the soldier. One part of this was to be a watchdog. Of the constellations of the icon, Canis Minor may have symbolized the duties of the Miles. The guardians in Plato's *Republic* may also have influenced this portion of Mithrasian iconography, since Platonic philosophy loomed large in the Roman World. In *The Republic*, the Guardians were likened to a watchdog, protecting the society in Plato's concept of an ideal state.

The Miles was given a more active role than the previous two degrees. The drossing process of Corax and the self-discovery of the Nymphus complete, the initiate now acquired a new personality. That is, the new focus of the self was energized. The first two degrees left behind the outer world, in the third, the candidate developed a new personality.

The Miles of Mithras probably served much as does the Tiler of the Royal Arch degree of the Freemasons. They functioned as guards, protecting the sanctity of the Mithraeum and the secrets of its theology. The job may have been considered ceremonial, since we don't have reports of Christians killing guards in order to destroy Mithraea, but the record may simply be incomplete in that regard.

Leo

Leo is the adept degree, the one at which the initiate enters the inner circle of the religion, or at least of the individual Mithraeum. Here the initiate learned the secrets of the religion, so it is not surprising that the Leo degree carries more associations than any other degree of the Mithrasian religion.

The importance of this degree as an adept degree should not be underestimated. For any initiatory group, the concept of Adept gives a portrait of the idealized human being. In Christianity, the popular view of angels provides this image; in the Mithrasian religion the statues of the lion-headed god do much the same.

The adept's planet was Jupiter, its constellations undoubtedly Leo, the lion, and Hydra, the snake. Its moral virtue was honesty and its element, fire. Its three devices were the fire shovel, the thunderbolt of Jupiter, and the sistrum.

The fire shovel reinforces Tertullian's description of the Leo as being of an arid or fiery nature.[4] For this same reason, the Leo washed his hands with honey rather than water; undoubtedly honey was placed on the Leo's hands and scraped off with a sturgil. This use of honey exactly paralleled the use of olive oil for washing hands, which was the common practice. It is notable, however, that honey was a much more expensive commodity.

The fire shovel, and perhaps the thunderbolt, too, was a symbol of stoking the fire and burning away one's mortal parts, thereby becoming entirely good and immortal. In this the Leo merely accepted a common motif of Greek and Roman myths and the Zarathustrian religion. In several myths, mortals become gods by being rubbed with ambrosia and then being placed in fire. The mortal parts burned, leaving the immortal parts to remain. Ambrosia's liquid form was nectar, and the association of nectar with both honey and ambrosia was commonplace in the ancient world. That this mythical motif was intended is attested to by the graffiti of the Aventine Mithraeum, which includes the following: "Accept, holy Father, the incense bearing Lions," and, "We offer through thee incense, through thee we are ourselves consumed."[5] In both cases the text affirms ritual as well as theology, and part of the theological implication is that Leo is consumed by the forces he has unleashed.

[4] Quoted in M. J. Vermaseren, *Mithras, The Secret God* (London: Chatto & Windus, 1959), p. 146. Also in R. L. Gordon, "Cumont and the Doctrines of Mithraism" in John R. Hinnells, *Mithraic Studies* (Manchester: Manchester University Press, 1975), p. 241; and John R. Hinnells, "Reflections on the Bull-Slaying Scene" in John R. Hinnells, *Mithraic Studies* (Manchester: Manchester University Press, 1975), p. 303.

[5] Quoted in M. J. Vermaseren, *Mithras, The Secret God*, p. 148 and 176. Also in John R. Hinnells, "Cumont and the Doctrines of Mithraism" in John R. Hinnells, *Mithraic Studies*, p. 241.

The thunderbolt was a symbol of rulership. Many Mithraea show paintings of Saturn handing the thunderbolt over to Jupiter, indicating the transfer of cosmic rulership to the latter god. The Mithraea also commonly show the use to which Jupiter put the bolts: attacking the giants. In one rewriting of the ancient myth, Jupiter attacked the giants with the thunderbolt for eating his son, Dionysus Zagreus. Afterward, Jupiter made the human race from the ashes of the defeated giants, and ever afterward human nature bore the mark of its origins: partly divine and partly chaotic, partly noble and partly bestial. In the degree of Leo, the noble part was said to have won the signal victory of gaining control over the chaotic side of the self.

The third device for the Leo degree was the sistrum, or rattle. This is normally associated with the religion of Isis, with which the Mithrasian religion clearly had a close connection.[6] The sistrum could have been used in several ways. It might have accompanied the chorus of Nymphae. In the confined spaces of the Mithraeum it might have been used to imitate thunder or, shaken lightly, the sound of buzzing bees, which themselves were a symbol of the soul incarnating. It is also possible the sistrum was a recognition that the Leo could "sound" the religion: carry its word and recruit new members. Any esoteric society must face the question of recruitment; clearly not all levels can do so. The pattern of recruitment in Mithrasism seems to have been nomination by a Leo and then acceptance by the Pater of the Mithraeum. In this Mithrasians would parallel the Masons.

The moral dimension of the Leo degree was truthfulness or honesty. This was not the lumpish, platitudinous attitude which passes for honesty today, but a burning, active force. With it came new duties and obligations within the religion. For once a Leo had his hands anointed with honey, he would have to keep them clean forever after. The Leo could never commit a crime nor touch con-

---

[6] Not only did a priest of Mithras assume a priesthood of Isis, several heads of statues or busts of Serapis have been found in Mithraea. Serapis is generally thought to be Osiris recast by the Ptolemaic dynasty, but as I hope to show at another time, he may actually have been Isis' virgin-born son.

taminated or evil objects. In the same way, the initiate's tongue was anointed with honey to indicate he must always speak the truth. Thus a Leo would always be scrupulously honest in word or deed.

The image of the lion, itself, reinforced this message because of its long association with courage and nobility, such as in the tales of Aesop. Similarly, on many lion-headed statues, the thunderbolt sits over the figure's heart, showing that the heart of the Leo had had its evil, bestial, or mortal parts burned away. There are many examples of lion-headed statues and the numerous additional devices associated with the degree, prime among them is the serpent, which winds around the body of the figure and rests its head on top of the figure's head. In some literature the coils are said to number seven to represent the seven planets, but the snake can be seen to coil around the human body anywhere from three to seven times. The number of coils may have been symbolically important in individual Mithraea, to individual members, or to individual artists, but there was no single theological purpose accepted by the whole of the religion. It is possible that the number of coils was in fact taken from the apparent coils of the constellation Hydra. Depending on how one counts, the zigzag line of stars forms anywhere from three to seven coils. At one point (near the star Alphard) the line actually doubles back. All the variations in representation of the snake in the lion-headed or lion-chested statues may derive from these characteristics of the constellation. For example, in a statue found at Sidon, the snake does not reach the lion's head, but instead forms one coil at the chest, just as the constellation doubles back on itself. But while the association with the constellations Leo and Hydra is clear, the theological intent of the variations is lost to us.

The lion-headed adept held two keys: the keys to heaven and earth. The Christians would later use the same symbolism for the Papacy, though in a different context. For Mithrasians, they were the keys to the ladder of salvation. On reaching this stage, the adept acquired a power of salvation not available to any lower degree, a power achieved by harnessing the nabarze, or holy energy, of life, salvation, and goodness that Mithras released when he slew the bull. For most it was an unconscious or hidden power. This unconscious wisdom, which often controls our actions, was symbolized by the snake coiled around the figure. The snake was an ancient symbol of wisdom and the unconscious, as it still is today. In some cases, it is a hindrance or a danger, as when the snake of the icon faces the scorpion; in others it leads to salvation, as when the snake approaches the wound of the bull or the mixing bowl.

Controlling one's thoughts, so important for members of the lower degrees to learn, suddenly becomes clearly necessary. Controlling thought was the "way" used in the religion to make members aware of (and to direct) the power represented by the snake. The snake, therefore, symbolized the power over which the adept gained control.

This symbolism applied to the bull-slaying scene as well as to the lion-headed statues. Not only were the statues entwined by snakes, but symbolism adorned the head and heart. The statues bore a lion's head in the same way that one of the three devices of every degree was worn on (or represented) the head; over the heart was placed a lion's head, a thunderbolt, or, in one case, an eye. The head and heart were clearly centers of occult power (or nabarze) in the Mithrasian religion, though the head took precedence over the heart.

That the snake rests its head on top of the figure shows that when the heart center became important, the head center was split into two natures—a higher and a lower. The Buddhist nature of this concept need not surprise us: in the first centuries of the Empire, Buddhism competed with other religions for converts. And like Mithrasism, Buddhism was accused of parodying the Christian rites before Christianity existed.

In addition to head and heart, there seem to have been other centers of occult power, or nabarze. A lion-headed statue from Castel Gandolfo has an eye on its chest and lion's heads on its knees and stomach; the figure is not entwined by a snake. A relief at Modena shows a "Phanes" version of the statue: human-headed, it hatches from a fiery egg and *is* entwined by a serpent. On its chest is a lion-head and on either side of the rib cage is a goat and a ram. The obvious allusion is to the zodiac—Lion–Leo, Ram–Aries, Goat–Capricorn. However, there is no discernible pattern to these signs. Another lion-headed statue was found which had zodiacal signs on the body, but only the torso was found; the rest is a modern reconstruction, which does not allow us to determine any other occult centers of power.

The probable additional centers of power, however, are the stomach, groin, knees, and feet. Of all these, the groin and feet are best attested to; in several cases, the Lion stands on a globe, emphasizing the power of the feet. But even if all are correct, the head and heart remain the main centers of nabarze or occult power in Mithrasism.

The lower head center (lion's head) was trained first, to begin a transformation of the candidate. The conscious thoughts, trained by exercises and ritual, opened up the heart (instinctive) and higher head (snake over the lion's head) centers of the soul. The candidate could then undergo more radical transformation. It was at this point that the thunderbolt took effect in the heart of the adept, who was "consumed"; his unworthy thoughts were destroyed, leaving behind only the divine elements of his soul. Thus the nabarze was released in the heart, head, and higher head centers, and possibly others. (It is interesting to note the centers described here— both known and theoretical—total seven, the same number as the seven degrees of the system.)

All this indicates the Leo must have been viewed as a person of considerable occult skills. This concept may have been symbolized by the representations of Saturn handing the thunderbolt, and hence power, to Jupiter. The Pater (subject to Saturn) granted the Leo (subject to Jupiter) a measure of occult or even political power; this may also have symbolized some form of "apostolic succession" which must have been essential to the Mithrasian system.

The occult power acquired by a Leo included the power to save his soul. The ladder of constellations between Cancer and Capricorn—birth and rebirth—was laid open to them. The Mithrasian

Leo had found the shortcut to salvation, and no longer had to use the long way round through the whole zodiac.

The Leo almost certainly also had occult power on this plane and in this life; graffiti indicates Leos were thought to have (or were hoped to have) fairly long lives. The exact range of magical powers of the Leos remains, however, unknown: perhaps the common range of magical practices of healing, luck charms, astral travel and divination were included. (The gems which have been found at several sites seem to have been used for magical rather than purely sacerdotal purposes.) Perhaps the tales of Mithrasians' legendary hardiness in the face of physical pain stems from their magical practices. We can't be certain because the texts are essentially silent on the point. Even Christian polemicists do not bear witness, which is somewhat different from saying there were no powers, since these practices would have remained within the inner circle of the religion—a circle into which Christianity never penetrated.

Perses

At some point in the development of every esoteric group, degrees cease to be a regular division designating teaching. Certain degrees become a combination of administrative functions and a recognition of the individual's own efforts to work with the teachings of the group. In the Golden Dawn, above the 5-6 degree of Adeptus Minor, certain administrative elements crept in. For example, a mother temple could only be formed by three people of the 7-4 Adeptus Exemptus degree or higher. Members of the three Adeptus grades, 5-6 to 7-4, were given a caucus of their own order within the general umbrella of the Golden Dawn. But at the same time, the higher degrees allowed for individual interpretation and initiative. When someone had completed the Adeptus Minor course, they had a grounding in most aspects of the Western-Semitic magical traditions. To put this to work on a personal level requires a profound effort on the part of any individual, an effort recognized by the higher degrees.

Mithrasism may have followed the same pattern. With the degree of Perses (and those above) we have in a sense not simply a Leo who joins other Leos, but a Leo who could lead other Leos. He could not only achieve an ecstatic state, but sustain it. His centers of power were not only open, they were controlled. They could not only be opened temporarily (as during the ritual), but kept open.

The degree Perses is fascinating if for no other reason than its name, which means Persian, is the name of the people whose empire was the only force able to match the armies of Rome. (It would seem rather like an American political party in the fifties having a leadership position called the Soviet.) However, as both Cumont[7] and Ulansey[8] have pointed out, the direct link may not be to the Persians in general, but to Perses, who was the son of Perseus. Perseus was thought to be the eponymous founder of the Persian race. If the son of Perseus were the sole model for the degree, however, many associations must have attached themselves to his name of which we are unaware.

The Perses degree is also interesting in that its planet is the Moon. Normally Luna was considered the proper planet of the first degree. The other degrees moved outward by their apparent distance from the Earth in a geocentric universe—Moon, Mercury, Venus, Sun, Mars, Jupiter, Saturn, and if used, the fixed stars. This is the pattern of the Tree of Life, the hidden pattern of the Hermetica,[9] and of Cicero's *Dream of Scipio*.[10] In the Mithrasian religion, however, the pattern is different—Mercury (Corax), Venus

---

[7] Franz Cumont, "Rapport sur une mission à Rome," in *Académie des Inscriptions et Belles-Lettres, Comptes Rendus* (Paris: Orientaliste Paul Geuthner, 1945), p. 418.

[8] David Ulansey, *The Origins of the Mithraic Mysteries: Cosmology and Salvation in the Ancient World* (Oxford: Oxford University Press, 1989), p. 38.

[9] Hermes Mercurius Trismegistus, *Divine Pymander*, ed. P. B. Randolph (1871; reprint, Mokelumne Hill, CA: Health Research, 1972), p 40. Paragraphs 59-68 indicate a series of vices to be discontinued which, taken in order, reflect the standard pattern of planetary concerns.

[10] Marcus Tullius Cicero, "The Dream of Scipio," in *On the Good Life*, trans. by Michael Grant (London: Penguin, 1971), pp. 346-347.

(Nymphus), Mars (Miles), Jupiter (Leo), Moon (Perses), Sun (Heliodromus), Saturn (Pater). The Moon and the Sun have been given a new place in the order.

The top three degrees may have had a special unity. They were all administrative, with special duties in ruling the Mithraeum. (The Perses wore a uniform consisting of a gray tunic, in itself a strong indication of the administrative function of the degree.) This would closely parallel the rule for Golden Dawn lodges, which also had three chiefs. It further recalls the system the early Romans borrowed from the Etruscans in which a temple was constructed to a triumvirate of gods: Jupiter, Juno, and Minerva was a common trio. The progression Moon-Sun-Saturn probably referred to the doorways of the souls and the path between them. The Moon referred to the closest door, Saturn the farthest. Between them was the Sun which was the traveller on the path until Mithras saved men through the shortcut.

The devices of the Perses degree were the Moon and eight-rayed star, the sickle, and the hooked sword. Each of these tells us something about the Perses' mystical role. Given the limitations of a mosaic as a medium, the star seems to be of the same type as seen on Cautes' and Cautopates' Phrygian caps and under Mithras' cloak in the Capua Mithraeum. There may have been a symbolic import to this star or it may simply have been an artistic convention.

Like the Leo, the Perses was anointed with honey. This was not because of his fiery nature, however, but rather to emphasize the preservative qualities of honey. The Perses was considered the "keeper of the fruits,"[11] a title which may refer to the job of treasurer. Honey was associated with the Moon, as were both bulls and bees. In the ancient world, bees were said to come from the hides of dead bulls, and were a symbol of the souls of people yet to be incarnated. The incarnated, in birth, passed through the doorway of the tropic of Cancer, the zodiacal sign ruled by the Moon.

The device of the sickle (or falx) is another reference to the Perses as "keeper of the fruits." The intimate connection of the

---

[11] Porphyry, quoted in Vermaseren, *Mithras*, p. 150.

Moon with the right times for planting and reaping, currently being rediscovered by an increasing number of modern farmers, was a universal canon in the ancient world. Moreover, in Zarathustrian theology, the diversity of the world's plants came as a result of the killing of the bull, an aspect of the event which doubtless entered Mithrasian mythology. The badge of the falx clearly indicated that the miracle of the slaying of the bull was ongoing.

The sword-with-a-hook, called a harpe, is a somewhat different case. Vermaseren gives the harpe as a scythe, which rather duplicates the falx. But the harpe was not a harvest tool, it was a weapon. In fact, it was the weapon Perseus used to behead the gorgon, Medusa. It seems likely that Perseus is here being alluded to not only by the name, but by the third device of the degree. The Romans, following Greek custom, liked eponymous solutions. The names of things were often assumed to come from a founder or inventor of the same or similar name. Thus the simple similarity of name gave the ancient Greeks the idea that Perseus somehow founded the Persian race—though the Iranians came to Persia before the Greeks came to Greece. Perseus, then, came after the Persians, whether he was a myth or history rewritten into myth. Perseus also had a son named Perses, whose association with the harpe may have completed an eponymous circle of the type which so delighted the ancient world.

Several constellations might have been the link of the degree of Perses to the Tauroctony, the image of Luna being the most obvious. But the figure of Luna is essentially subsidiary in the Tauroctony, where she is portrayed as a conventional balance to her brother, the Sun or Sol. The Moon does not appear as a figure in her own right in the scene, but rather as an artistic convention used for balance; a counterpoint to the Sun and a development of the Cautes-Cautopates pair. Crater the mixing bowl may also refer to Perses' title of keeper of the fruits. But the bowl is also a secondary figure in the Tauroctony, and is connected more closely to the lion, without whom it never appears.

The image of the icon best connected to Perses is the bull. The bull is directly associated with the Moon, as well as with bees, and they in turn are both associated with the souls of those who will incarnate through the zodiacal gate of the Moon. The fruits the Perses keeps represent the souls of the members of the community. His duty, symbolized by the honey, is the preservation of those souls.

Heliodromus

The Heliodromus functioned as the deputy of the Pater, taking over in the event of his temporary incapacity. He, like the Perses, had administrative duties, as indicated by the official dress of the degree. A painting at the St. Prisca Mithraeum shows a Heliodromus wearing a red garment with a yellow belt, holding a blue globe and greeting a Pater.

The Heliodromus was the representative of the Sun-god in this world. In reenactments of the Sacred Meal, he played the part of the god, just as the Pater took the place of Mithras. In St. Prisca again a mural representation of the Sacred Meal of Mithras and Sol survives in which Sol wears the same garments as the Heliodromus and Mithras wears the same as the Pater. So the connection between the Heliodromus and Sol is absolute. In the Tauroctony, the image of the Sun likewise represented this degree.

The devices of the Heliodromus are the whip the Sun-god used to spur the four horses pulling his chariot, the nimbus that appeared around the Sun-god's head, and the torch. Each had an occult meaning. There is an exercise in the occult known as putting on the god form, in which an individual spends a long period exploring all they can learn about a particular god. This includes reading and re-reading the myths of the god, examining the various objects of worship of the god, and anything else pertaining to that deity. When they have brought themselves to a critical point, they try to mold their own astral body in the image of the deity.

This seems to be the occult intent of the degree of the Heliodromus. The individual Heliodromus—there seems to have been only one per Mithraeum—focused his own magical energies, his nabarze, to become the ecstatic representative of the god Sol. This explains the important position that Sol seemed to hold in the religion of Mithras. The deity is represented in many Mithraea, his image second in frequency only to Mithras and the bull-slaying scene.

Sol appears in various poses and roles. Sometimes he is standing; sometimes he drives his chariot. He appears in many bull-slaying scenes, a ray of light shooting from him to Mithras, who turns his head to regard Sol's light and his messenger, the raven.

In the religion which bears his name, Mithras replaced Sol as the power of the universe. But Sol, though diminished, was in no way vanquished. He still remained an important force. And just as he gave his message to the raven, so his deputy the Heliodromus gave the Coraxes the message of Mithrasism.

Pater

The Pater was the head of the Mithraeum, and no Mithraeum could last long without a Pater. The main strength of the Paters was in the local Mithraeum, where they not only presided over the community, they were a part of the continuum of degrees. In that, at least, the Pater was very much the same as any other member. He was the nerve center of the religion and a repository of magical training, as indicated by his many titles. He was Pater, or father, to the fratres, or brothers, who made up the general membership; he was the high priest (*summus pontifex*) of the religion; he was chosen by his fellow Paters (*consacranei syndexi*) according to the law (*pater nominus*) to be the defender (*defensor*) of the mysteries.

The position of Pater was sacerdotal, requiring specialist knowledge, as well as administrative abilities. One item of graffiti shows that a Pater had to have studied astrology to attain his degree, indicating that a Pater faced a preliminary time of training, and a specific system of testing. At the Aventine Mithraeum in Rome, which served as a kind of Papal See to the religion, the distinction between the sacerdutal and administrative facets of the position are made clear. The differences between a *Pater Sacrorum* and a *Pater Patrum* are reinforced by the use of two different names. The first meant Pater of the Sacred. It would seem his duties were to guide theological development and maintain ritual purity. In this his role would closely parallel the Persian Magi of the religion of Zarathustra. Vermaseren[12] also suggests that this Pater was responsible for initiation and the acceptance of new members. He may have overseen this, but the religion was scattered over too wide an area for one man to deal with individual candidates for each degree.

According to graffiti, the *Pater Patrum* ("Father of Fathers") was chosen from among ten superiors (*dedacam primus*), a system rather like that of a Pope chosen by the college of cardinals, or the Master of the Templars, who was always responsible to his own council of nobles who elected him and who would elect his successor. No evidence survives as to how vacancies on the council were filled. It is possible the councilors were chosen by the *Pater Patrum*, as in the case of the Papacy and the Knights Templar. This, however, implies that the executive position—Pope, Master, or *Pater Patrum*—carried a life tenure. Any need to re-elect the head would soon make the system be, and quickly be seen to be, irredeemably corrupt.

Nor is it clear whether the *Pater Patrum* was elected from among the council of ten of which he continued to be a member, or whether his tenure on the council ceased with election. In other words, we don't know whether there was a *Pater Patrum and* a council of ten, or a *Pater Patrum* who, with nine others, *formed* a council of ten. It seems most likely that the *Pater Patrum* was raised in distinction above his fellow council members. This would follow a number of conventions. The individual Mithraea were headed by a single Pater. The Empire in which the Mithrasian religion flourished was run by an Emperor who had a Senate of

[12] Vermaseren, *Mithras*, p. 153.

which he was not a member. And in the legions of the Empire, the commandant of troops was not a member of a council. The Mithrasians, however, may have been led by a *Pater Patrum* who had a council of ten, one of whom was the *Pater Sacrorum*. This council of superiors may have been the core of the groups sent out to check on individual Mithraea.

The office of Pater carried certain moral requirements. The Pater must be pious—one of his titles was pientissimus (most pious), just as the highest degree of the Golden Dawn was ipsissimus (most wholly oneself). That is, the Pater was most wholly pious in the way the Golden Dawn led one to become most wholly oneself.

The Pater also had to have some courage, as his title defensor (defender) shows. Some Paters seem to have paid the ultimate price of their office, the chained skeleton of one found murdered by Christians on the altar of his god attests to this.

A Pater must also be dignified, as required by his title of dignissimus. Certainly the painting at Dura-Europas shows the Pater with a most dignified mien. In Dura-Europas, another title of a Pater appears, that of "autopatros," which Vermaseren[13] takes to be perhaps a preliminary grade to that of Pater. It is true this would be the same practice as the Golden Dawn preliminary grades; the Neophyte grade was in fact preliminary to full membership in the order. And there was a "link" grade before a member became an Adeptus Minor (or Theoricus Adeptus Minor, to be more accurate).

But if we look to the common Roman practice, particularly within the military there is another explanation. The term "autopatros" may refer to the normal provincial development. It may indicate an "autonomous Pater," perhaps the equivalent of an archbishop. This suggestion is supported by certain graffiti in Rome, which contain the names of a number of non-Latin merchants usually thought to be Syrian merchants who came to Rome with the Severan dynasty. Several of the Emperors, and many of the

[13] Vermaseren, *Mithras*, p. 153.

nobles, of that dynasty were Mithrasians, so it is quite in keeping with normal practice to grant special favors—religious and secular—to home provinces. In this case the autopatros would be part of a developing administrational structure much like the one Christianity would eventually adopt.

At the head of this administration was the Pater Patrum leading his council of ten, one of whom may have been the Pater Sacrorum. Regions such as Syria, and perhaps later the Danube, each gained an autopatros with as-yet unknown powers and duties. Under them were the Patres of the various Mithraea. Given that the Pater had such a central role, both administratively and occultly, the Mithrasian religion is likely to have had some form of apostolic succession. Such a succession would not only have strengthened the central administration, it would also have ensured that clear standards of training were maintained.

The planet of the Pater degree is Saturn. The Pater's three devices of office are the Phrygian cap of Mithras, the staff and ring (which I take to be one item) and the hooked sword or sickle. In pictures, we see the Pater dressed as Mithras, for he was Mithras' deputy on earth. Likewise he is associated with Mithras in the Tauroctony. His constellation is either Perseus or Orion, depending on whether one follows Ulansey or Speidel. It is possible the Danubian region preferred the constellation of Orion, while Syria preferred Perseus.

The hooked sword or sickle refers to Saturn, just as the whip and nimbus relate the Heliodromus directly to the Sun-god and the crescent relates Perses to the Moon. The sickle was the weapon Saturn used to castrate his father, Ouranous, and thereby usher in the golden age. In Mithrasian representations, Saturn transfers his power to Jupiter by a treaty, rather than Jupiter usurping it, as in the classic myth. Thus for Mithrasians, Saturn symbolized the change of ages, as did Mithras himself.

Saturn and the Pater degree are closely indentified. Both dealt with the shedding of blood. Both bear symbols connected with the genitals—Saturn, castration, and Mithras, the scorpion. Both deities represent a change of ages.

The staff and ring were symbols of authority that survive to-day in the bishop's ring of office and his shepherd's crook. Interestingly, the hook of the Pater's sickle, attached to his staff, would make the Pater's symbols the same as the bishop's. The Phrygian cap was the same as Mithras' own, symbolizing the belief that the Pater had achieved a special identification with the god, thus completing a process begun as a Corax. Stiffened, with its folded top changed into a split, this cap became the bishop's miter, another symbol of the Pater transferred into the new religion. But, though the outer form of the devices of the Pater were subsumed by Christianity, their deeper meaning was not. The bishop may have borrowed the symbols of the Pater, but not the occult initiation.

Chryfii

Inscriptions at Rome mention the "Chryfii" or "Cryfii," which means "hidden ones." It has been suggested the term refers to the Nymphus and the veil associated with that grade. It has also been suggested to refer to the children of members who were not yet ready for initiation.

The inscription is quite late in the religion's history at Rome, being dated to the fourth century. The two inscriptions simply state two Paters initiated several people into special grades, "osterderunt cryfios" and "tradiderunt chryfios." The possibility arises that the terms refer to those given the special mission of sending the movement underground.

Were the two Paters trying to avoid the persecution of Mithrasism by Constantine and the Christians by creating a secret membership? This would, after all, be very much what the Christians are said to have done for four centuries of their existence.

Chapter Six

The Rituals of Mithras

The Tauroctony was the religious core of Mithrasism; the degrees were its earthly reflection. But the Mithrasians were blessed not only with a theology (now lost), but a series of rituals (almost lost). Indeed, conversion to the Mithrasian religion was itself a ritual of initiation as was the passage through the degrees. An examination of the archaeological evidence and some comments by enemies can provide some understanding of the ritual life of the Mithrasians.

The Sacred Meal

I believe the Sacred Meal took two forms, a full meal and a communion. The full meal itself included cooked meat, fruit, bread and wine. The communion included only bread and wine.

The two forms of the Sacred Meal may have arisen for any number of reasons. It may have been the cost of meat and fruit simply became too much for some members. It is also possible the rituals were differentiated for theological reasons. The existence of a briefer, less elaborate communion may, for instance, have helped to heighten the solemnity of the occasions on which the full Sacred Meal was served. But I would suggest the division arose as a natural outgrowth of the degree system. The evidence indicates that the roles of the different degrees changed when the different rituals were performed. In the full Sacred Meal, only the Leos and their superiors have significant parts to play (except that the Coraxes are given waitering jobs). In the more general, less elaborate communion all degrees participate.

Justin, one of the Christian polemicists, admits the Mithrasians use bread and water in their rituals. Tertullian admits the Sacred Meal of the Mithrasians is a "devilish imitation" of the Christian sacrament.[1] Most modern writers agree Justin is saying water to cover up the use of wine. Justin also admits certain formulas were used, and these were comparable to the Christian ritual of the Eucharist. Murals showing the communion show bread being used, and that bread is sometimes in the form of wafers or small cakes with a cross on them.

In one or both meals there is a procession of members of the Leo degree. If nothing else, it probably tells us a Mithraeum needed at least four Leos to function, so the minimum number must have been a Pater, a Heliodromus, a Perses, and four Leos—seven members. The first Leo carries a lit taper in one hand and an armload of spares. It seems his job was to light the lamps of the Mithraeum. The second Leo carries a cock, no doubt to be sacrificed, and perhaps to supply a meal for the members of the community. The third Leo, called "Phoebus" or "shining," carries a bowl in which is a loaf of bread or a cake. The fourth, called "Gelasius" or "laughing," carries a vessel of wine.

These men are shown as bringing their offerings to the gods Sol and Mithras, who sit at the head of the Mithraeum. The Sacred Meal and communion, after all, commemorated events in their god's life, but possibly different events. Mithras and Sol are often shown as reclining together at a meal. In recreations of this event on Earth, the Pater represented Mithras and the Heliodromus represented Sol.

But in paintings of Mithras and Sol dining together, however, only wine and bread are shown, meat is not. Possibly the end of

---

[1] Both Justin and Tertullian are quoted in M. J. Vermaseren, *Mithras, The Secret God* (London: Chatto & Windus, 1959), p. 103. The same two authors are also discussed and quoted, with rather different conclusions, in J. P. Kane, "The Mithraic Cult Meal" in *Mithraic Studies*, ed. John R. Hinnells (Manchester: Manchester University Press, 1975), pp. 315-316.

the meal is shown, when the meat has been consumed, the compact secure, and the new order of the heavens established. For example, a relief at Heddernheim shows Sol offering grapes to Mithras, while Mithras holds a drinking horn. The skin of the sacrificed bull lies below them. Behind them, their hats are set together with the nimbus radiant from Mithras' cap. Other representations of the Sacred Meal of bread and wine show more detail. In the Konjic relief for instance, the Pater and the Heliodromus partake of wine and small cakes or loaves of bread marked with a cross. A Corax, Perses, Miles, and Leo all come to the altar to receive the blessed bread and wine, which are the flesh and blood of salvation. Each member brings his own drinking horn, probably a symbol of Mithras' hunting exploits.

The communion probably celebrates the meal of Mithras and Sol. Before that meal, an oath was sworn. Like the oaths of the ancient Aryans, it was sworn before a fire; like the treaty between the Mitanni and the Hittites, it was sworn between Mithras and a sun-god. A painting of this scene in the Mithraeum at Palazzo Barberini in Rome shows Mithras and Sol holding a small spit on the altar of the oath. A relief from Poetovio shows them shaking hands over a fire altar. Above their hands is a spit filled with small pieces of meat. A raven pecks at the meat, perhaps a reference to Coraxes as not only waiters but opportunists. The Perses may have been given the job of controlling the Coraxes during the ceremonies. In another version of the meal, the Leos recline and are served by the Coraxes. The Pater and Heliodromus take their normal places in or near the nave. The Coraxes look on and aspire to the achievement of the Leos.

At the full Sacred Meal quite a bit of meat seems to have been consumed, including beef, pork, mutton, and fowl, to judge from the pits of bones left near Mithraea. This and the wine may easily have become expensive over time, leading to the ritual occurring only once a month, probably on the sixteenth. In the Persian calendar, the sixteenth was sacred to Mithra, and this practice probably continued in Rome with Mithras. On other days, the briefer, less elaborate communion would be given. This may have occurred weekly, but it is possible that the lesser communion was performed every day with different groups of members participating in a kind of roster.

Initiation

Membership in the religion and advancement through its various degrees was essential for the soul to progress. Each step along the path was marked by an initiation ritual about which we have a number of scraps of information. Unfortunately, not enough information survives to reconstruct every ritual in its entirety.

Moreover, some of the textual evidence is unreliable, being part of an organized polemic by a rival creed. One sixth century Christian writer—which is to say someone writing less than a century after Christianity's triumph—gave as ordeals faced by Mithrasians as a fifty day fast, two days of chafing, and twenty days of being left in snow. An eighth century writer said there were eighty tests, including submersion in water for several days, being put into fire, solitary life and fasting.[2] Fortunately when we have removed the fantasies there are some elements of the rituals of which we can be certain.

We know from Tertullian[3] that anyone seeking initiation into Mithrasism first had to undergo a period of instruction, after which the candidate presented himself to the Pater of the Mithraeum. If accepted, he would then be initiated into the community and become a frater.

According to a fourth century text, at his initiation into the mysteries, the candidate was bound with chicken guts and blindfolded.[4] He was then made to leap, or was thrown, over a ditch filled with water. A man would then approach the candidate with a sword and cut his bonds. The man with the sword was called the Liberator. We don't know if any continuing relationship of patronage existed between the Liberator and candidate. Sometime be-

[2] Both authors are quoted in Vermaseren, *Mithras*, p. 134.
[3] Tertullian, *Apology,* chapter 8, quoted in Vermaseren, *Mithras*, p. 129.
[4] Quoted in Vermaseren, *Mithras*, p. 133.

fore, during, or after this initiatory sequence, the candidate swore an oath to protect the secrets of the religion. Most writers assume this occurred before the ritual. That, however, would constitute a most unusual occult practice, since an oath taken during an initiation has more force than a promise made before or after.

During the initiation the candidate may have been branded or tattooed on the wrist. Soldiers of Rome were normally branded on the wrist to prevent desertion. In their case it is possible that no additional mark was added. Merchants and others may have been branded, but for soldiers, attention was probably just drawn to the existing brand.

The Mithraeum at Capua contains scenes of initiation, although it is not known if they represent a membership ritual or passage through the various degrees. Probably these are other scenes in that first initiation. If so they indicate a series of trials faced by the candidate.

In all scenes the candidate is naked, which may explain something of the exclusion of women. In one of the scenes an officer of the rite, dressed in a white tunic with red borders (the same uniform that would later be used by the Golden Dawn), is pushing the candidate forward by the shoulders. The candidate is blindfolded; his hands are before him. The candidate's attitude seems to be one of uncertainty. He raises his arms from his sides and holds them before him, but not at a level you would expect if he were in fact using them to ward off or discover obstacles. Instead they seem raised in uncertainty. The candidate is being pushed forward, not knowing where he is going. One can almost imagine the Leos on their benches, heightening the fear of the candidate with an occasional gasp as if the candidate were about to meet some unpleasant fate. The candidate, forced to move forward blindly, would be in a highly anxious state, his most primitive fears brought to the fore.

Perhaps the candidate is brought to a ditch filled with water. Although the texts describe one, the murals at Capua don't show such a ditch. In the second scene at Capua the candidate kneels, blindfolded, with his hands behind his back. He may be bound. The man in white stands before him, while a Pater approaches from behind carrying a sword or stick. This may be a depiction of the role of Liberator, described above. In the third image, however, it appears that the Pater (or other red-cloaked priest) gives the white-robed official the object, which is probably a sword.

In the third scene the candidate kneels on one knee. His hands are still behind his back and he is still blindfolded. The officer of the initiation stands behind him with his arms outstretched and his hands behind the candidate's head—a stance well known to ritual occultists as the projection of power. The sword lies next to the candidate. It indicates the transfer, which was no doubt accompanied by an oath or description of the sword's mystic purpose. Other people are present at this stage of the ritual but we are not certain of their role, due in part to the poor condition of the painting.

The last mural of the series shows the candidate with his hands crossed over his chest in what ritual occultists call the Osiris position. The candidate is on both knees, the white-robed officer is standing behind him. The officer's left hand holds the candidate's left hand over the candidate's right shoulder. The officer's right hand is crossed over his arm and is reaching for or releasing the candidate's right hand over the candidate's left shoulder. The scene recalls not only the Osiris position, but the various grips used by Masons and the Golden Dawn. The position, while impractical as an actual handshake, served as a kind of mudra, and doubtless had an esoteric meaning.

Just in front of the candidate is a circular object which may be a wreath or a loaf of bread. Believing this not to be a representation of the third degree initiation (Miles) but rather initiation into the religion or as a Corax, I suggest it is a loaf of bread. A red-cloaked Pater is holding a sword pointed at the bread, a common means of infusing magical power into an object such as a talisman or, in this case, bread to be eaten.

A ninth century writer, Suidas,[5] supplies an interesting fact about the initiation and its trials. If the candidate did not pass the trials, he could not be admitted to the Mithrasian religion. Given this fact, and using patterns found in other initiatory groups as

---

[5] Quoted in Vermaseren, *Mithras*, pp. 133-134.

models, we can attempt to reconstruct the initiation into Mithrasism. That is, we can compose a palimpsest of the script the Mithrasians themselves may have used.

(1) The potential member is brought to the notice of the Leos at a full Sacred Meal. If seconded and approved, he is approached.

(2) If the potential member is willing, he is taught the "open secrets" of the religion. This would include much that was generally available but which was incorporated into the religion in a special way. For example, the signs of the zodiac and the rulership of planets might have been taught. Of Mithras, much could have been said: he was a god of light who by a brave act brought salvation to those who follow his path. The nature of this salvation (e.g., rebirth or entrance into an Elysium) would have been explained. Undoubtedly much would have been made of Mithras' ancient past in Persia. The Romans not only admired, but were awed by the ancient wisdom of the Orient.

(3) If the potential member has learned his lessons well, he is presented to the Pater of the Mithraeum to be questioned. If he fails this test, he is turned away. If he passes, he is initiated.

(4) During the night of the Sacred Meal, initiations are performed, a fact inferred from Christian polemic which describes the binding used as chicken gut, and the murals which show a chicken brought in procession for sacrifice. The symbolism of the cock's crow driving away evil spirits is also plain here.

(5) At some point the candidate is brought into the Mithraeum. In the anteroom, he is disrobed and blindfolded.

(6) A man in a white tunic with red borders—possibly the man who offered the candidate for admission—puts his hands on the candidate's shoulders and pushes him forward. Possibly sounds are used to enhance the fear the candidate feels.

(7) An oath is administered to the candidate to reveal nothing of what he may see or hear in the Mithraeum. If the candidate accepts the oath, he is bound with the guts of a sacrificed cock—symbolically "bound" to the force of light.

(8) Still blindfolded and unworthy to see what surrounds him, the candidate is forced to kneel. In this position he is presented to the Pater. The Pater brings a sword which is given to the offic-

er. An oath or exchange must have occurred explaining the significance of the sword, most likely a description of the slaying of the bull.

(9) The sword is laid beside the candidate and magical energy (nabarze) is passed from the officer of the initiation to the candidate. In this the whole of the religion may have possessed a concept like that of the priestly apostolic succession of the Roman Catholic and Anglican churches.

(10) The sword is taken and the bonds of the candidate are cut. They could not be cut before the receipt of nabarze. However, the candidate still seeks the light and is thus left blindfolded.

(11) The candidate is then forced to both knees and his arms put in the Osiris position. The officer crosses his own arms, taking the candidate's left hand in his left and right hand in his right.

(12) While this is happening, a loaf of bread is put before the candidate and blessed with the sword, showing the bread as the flesh of the bull which is meant to give salvation to the followers of the religion.

(13) Since the candidate is being restrained from being able to take the bread (which implies fasting before this initiation), there must be some discussion or explanation of the significance of the bread made flesh and the wine made blood.

(14) At this stage, the candidate is put to a test. He may have been rebound and thrown over a pit of water, but if so no trace of these pits has been found. Some test must have occurred.

(15) If the test is passed, the blindfold is removed and the bread eaten. If not, the candidate is refused admission to the religion and sent out. The culmination, then, was removing the blindfold so the candidate could see the bull-slaying scene of the icon in the east, as a full member of the religion and known as a frater (brother).

Advancement Through the Degrees

As members advanced through the ranks, other rituals marked their progress. To judge from the Golden Dawn and Freemasonry, these rituals were neither as spectacular nor as long as the membership ritual, and our knowledge of them is scanty. Entrance into each degree must have had an element of investiture to it. The symbols of the degrees shown in the floor mosaic in the Mithraeum at Ostia show us three items associated with each grade, which leads to the inference that the initiation described above admitted the candidate to the religion itself, not to the first degree of Corax.

Fire shovels belonging to members of the Leo degree have survived. They are ornately made, with zodiacal and other cosmic symbols on them. These are the only implements of investiture found—no mirror of a Nymphus, for example, has been found. But where implements have ritual purpose, as they undoubtedly did in Mithrasism, they must inevitably be blessed, sanctified, and given to the recipient with all due ceremony and oath. This no doubt happened as members advanced through each of the degrees of the Mithrasian religion. But different degrees had different emphases so we'll examine them separately.

1. Corax

A candidate for Corax would ritually receive a caduceus, a cup, and a raven. This last may have been a raven's mask, some feathers, or a live bird. At each stage, a recitation occurred of the individual member's accomplishments. For example: "Corax, under the tutelage of Mercury you have labored to understand the lessons put before you. You have learned to struggle against the darkness in yourself, to awaken to the light in you by the moral lesson of humility...."

2. Nymphus

A candidate for Nymphus or bride was no doubt presented with a veil, a mirror, and a lamp, all three indicating reflection. One inscription implies that the members of the Nymphus grade had to sing, so perhaps they formed part of a sacred choir. Vermaseren[6] also suggests that, during the rite of initiation to this degree, the Mithraeum was flooded with light. If so, the passage from Corax to Nymphus was seen as from darkness or semi-darkness to light.

[6] Vermaseren, *Mithras*, p. 143.

3. Miles

To enter the degree of Miles the candidate faces his first test. The ritual officer presents him with a laurel wreath perched on the edge of a sword and then places the wreath on his head. The candidate must push it off with the flat of his hand, declaring to the group that Mithras alone is victory and he will not again wear a wreath. The wreath is then placed on his shoulder. The wreath on the tip of a sword recalls the Ace of Swords in the Tarot; the refusal of a wreath recalls Caesar's refusal of a crown.

But this refusal was not only a private one, confined to the walls of the Mithraeum. The Miles had to refuse accolades in public. Thus from at least this degree the individual Mithrasian was to publicly declare his allegiance to Mithras, much as the Christians did to Christ. But where Christians refused to swear to the Emperor, the Mithrasians merely refused his accolades. The Miles initiation is also the first ritual in which the candidate knows his role ahead of time—that is, the candidate is no longer merely the subject of the ritual but also a participant in it, however briefly.

Some sources claim that the Miles was branded on the forehead, though it seems more likely the candidate was anointed with ash or clay. Roman soldiers were commonly branded on the wrist; Emperors placed similar brands on their coins. But because you can't show a branded wrist on a coin, they showed the brand on the forehead instead. As in the army, the anointing or ritual "brand" declared the Miles forever in the service of his god and showed that he placed his god at the center of his own life.

The degree of Miles carried another ritual duty: bearing the train of higher initiates, particularly Leos, during ceremonies. The Miles thus has gained a new status, one enjoyed fully with advancement to the next degree.

4. Leo

As a Leo, the candidate becomes an adept, with all that implies. Every esoteric group possesses a degree at which the emphasis changes from tutelage to the exercise of authority, a degree at which the candidate completes his studies and accomplishes a reorientation of his inner psyche. In the case of the Adeptus Minor degree of the Golden Dawn or the Royal Arch degree of the Freemasons, the ceremony suddenly becomes more dramatic at this point. New symbolism is presented and new kinds of oaths taken. The Leo degree of the Mithrasians follows this pattern.

At his initiation, the Leo still receives the devices of his rank: the fire shovel, the sistrum, and the thunderbolt. Illustrations also tend to show Leos wearing red cloaks, or white robes with red trim. The color red clearly had some connection with the degree, probably symbolizing the connection of the degree to the element fire. In Africa, a statue of the lion-headed god was hollowed out so fire could spit from his mouth. Porphyry[7] claims the candidate for the Leo degree had to be baptized by fire. His words imply this is a ritual presaging a future conflagration—the end of the world by fire. This was a common belief in the Greek and Roman worlds from about the fifth century B.C.E. It was also integral to Zarathustrian religious views of Mithra.

This fiery apocalypse is also alluded to in the Leo's ritual of initiation, in which the candidate is placed in a chamber roughly the size of a bathtub, and subjected to alternate extremes of heat and cold.

When the Leo arises from the tub, he is presented ritually as having risen from the dead, possibly at the end of the world. This would explain the enactment of resurrection that some ancient writers mention; perhaps the intention was to assume the Miles had died in the service of his god, and been resurrected as a Leo. In some cases the lion-headed statues have been modeled on Roman grave guardians.

Undoubtedly at this stage, the full meaning of the "lion-headed god" statues and the bull-slaying scene is given to the initiate in a ceremony similar to the knowledge lectures of the Golden Dawn and the tracing board lectures of Masons. And at this point the new Leo probably learns of his new duties, including bringing gifts of incense, sacrificial animals, and votive statues to Mithras, either directly or through the Pater.

[7] Quoted in Vermaseren, *Mithras*, p. 148.

Enough evidence exists in the case of the Leo to allow a reasonably accurate reconstruction of the initiation ritual.

(1) The candidate enters the Mithraeum with the kitbag, lance, and helmet of a Miles, but is divested of these as the assembly laments the loss of one who died in the service of the god of light.

(2) On the basis you take nothing with you when you die except what lies within your heart, the candidate is stripped and placed naked in a confined chamber about the size of a bathtub, which symbolizes the "tomb."

(3) Here he is subjected to extremes of cold and heat as a liturgy is read describing the end of the world. The myth involves terrible cold, followed by terrible heat, rivers of fire, and other elements familiar from both Greek and Persian mythology. Both Norse pagans and Zarathustrians believed the end of the world would be preceded by three winters without intervening summer; the Mithrasians may have believed the same. Since the dead were thought to understand the passing of events, this part of the ritual may have represented a kind of dress rehearsal for the candidate's own personal death.

(4) After the reading of the liturgy, the candidate is raised from the tomb and given the tools of the Leo: the sistrum, the fire shovel, and the thunderbolt. Each is explained as it is received. He also receives a red robe or cloak, symbolizing that he has immersed himself in fire, which has "consumed" his evil or mortal parts.

(5) An initiate of a higher degree then explains the lion-headed statues and the Tauroctony, and gives the secret of the stellar explanation of the icon. This explanation moves one step beyond the mythology presented to members of lower degrees as an explanation of the rites.

(6) The Leo is now cleansed with honey. He has been reborn and so undergoes the same rituals Romans practiced on newborn children. Henceforth, every sin committed is considered far worse than those committed earlier in life. This cleansing is symbolized by pouring honey over the candidate's hands. Similarly, honey is placed on the candidate's tongue to cleanse it of sin. The new Leo must maintain the good of Mithras in every word and deed, and

keep the word of Mithras in his heart, carrying out the Zarathustrian injunction to live by "good thoughts, good words, good deeds." To sin after initiation constituted an unforgivable act, for the Leo would do so in full knowledge of what he was doing.

5. Perses

Very little information survives concerning the initiation into the Perses degree. This I have suggested since it was an administrative degree. We know the Perses is presented with honey, not as a cleansing agent, but because he is the guardian of it: "the keeper of the fruits." No doubt he is also presented with the devices of office. The candidate may also receive the badge of office and, if so, is told of its uses. But more than this we do not know.

6. Heliodromus

Nothing survives of the initiation into this degree, either. But the devices of office are not those one would receive in the course of an initiation. I therefore think it likely that initiation into the degree of Heliodromus took the form of a stage play. In this play the candidate must have played the role of the Sun-god in the relationship between Sol and Mithras. Thus the candidate would have had to submit to the Pater as Sol did to Mithras, through the ritual pact of blood brotherhood, oath over an altar, or other elements familiar through the murals which decorated the Mithraea.

7. Pater

We know nothing of the initiation rites of the Pater. We do know, though, that preparation to be a Pater involved significant studies, including astrology, as we can tell from one graffiti description. But he no doubt also had to learn the rituals of the religion, its various initiations, its holidays, and its theology. Only then could he be fit to bestow initiation to new members. Once the training was over, some form of ceremony must have occurred; at the very least the Pater must have been invested with the ring and staff, the sickle, and his ceremonial outfit.

Mithrasmas & Others

The last kind of ritual of which we have knowledge are the holidays and special events of Mithrasism. We know, for example, at the establishment or refurbishment of a Mithraeum animals were sacrificed and undoubtedly then consumed at a Sacred Meal.

The Mithrasians also seem to have celebrated the festival of Pales, a member of the traditional Roman pantheon. Her festival was held on April 21st each year, and was called the Palilia. This celebration required the purification of sheep on the eve of the festival. The sheep were washed, and their pens cleaned and garlanded. On the day of the festival, the statue of the goddess Pales was sprinkled with milk and prayers were addressed to it asking for forgiveness and blessings. Following the prayer people leaped over a fire and were cleansed or purified with water.

It was a celebration that fit well with the belief in a past flood and a coming conflagration of fire, a belief which must have permeated the Mithrasian religion.

On December 25th, the Mithrasians celebrated the birth of their god, and had done so since before Jesus was supposed to have been born. The Mithrasians, though, also celebrated the equinoxes.

How they did this we do not know. It has been suggested, though, that Mithrasmas—the birth of Mithras—may have been celebrated by presents (taken from the traditional Roman Saturnalia) and decorating a pine tree with candles.

It would seem almost certain they arranged a nativity scene of the birth of Mithras. The nave of the Mithraeum would have been an ideal place to arrange this, various members of the community taking the role of shepherds for a nativity play. The shepherds were attracted by the sacred light and the divine messenger appeared to tell them the significance of what was happening. They approached the divine child and worshipped the one who would, by his action of sacrifice, save the souls of the human race.

The ritual celebrations of Palilia and Mithrasmas undoubtedly also included reconstructions of the mythic events of Mithras' life, including the Sacred Meal, Mithras' last supper before ascending to heaven. Chapter 7 relates some of the more important events in the life of Mithras.

Chapter Seven

The Life and Myths of Mithras

The walls of the Mithraea give eloquent testimony to the mythic life of Mithras. In the same way, Christians put events of the life of Jesus on the walls of their churches to serve symbolic purpose, and to be a guide to the faithful. In the same way, the Mithrasians drew strength and guidance from representations of the events in life of Mithras.

Again, like the reliefs in Christian churches with which we are familiar, some of these events are capable of imitation in the individual follower's life, some are raw material for allegory, and others cannot be imitated at all by mortal beings.

The Holy Birth

Mithras was born on December 25th, the day of the winter solstice on the old calendar (now it's the 22nd). The date was a very deliberate reference to the solar year, since we know from graffiti that Mithras bore the secret name Meitras, which in Greek numerology has a value of 365.

Mithras was born from a rock, a divine light and fire emanating either from him or from the rock. Of his conception, we know nothing. He is shown naked except for the Phrygian cap sometimes placed on his head. He holds a dagger in one hand—probably the dagger with which he will slay the bull. In the other hand, normally his left, he may hold any one of a number of objects: a globe of dominion over the world, a torch, a bow and arrow(s), or sheaves of wheat. These all represent some aspect of Mithras' role as god.

Many attendants appear at the divine birth. Shepherds are often shown, sometimes with sheep and goats, but never with cattle, implying that Mithras emerged when men had domesticated sheep, but not cattle. His association with cattle must have been a later accretion or the time of his birth is truly arcadian.

The shepherds are attracted to the site by the light and fire that accompanies the birth—perhaps a reference to the discovery of flint. A divine messenger, Mercury or Saturn, appears to tell them the significance of the event. The shepherds arrive at the point at which Mithras' birth is either just complete or almost completed. In some representations, the shepherds assist at the birth by pulling Mithras out by his arms.

Gods also attend the birth. Cautes and Cautopates are sometimes shown, like the shepherds, performing midwifery for the young god. Other deities sometimes attend the birth of Mithras, chiefly Saturn.

Saturn never plays an active role in these scenes. He normally reclines against a rock, sometimes with a dagger in his hand, as if to pass this on to Mithras. In some cases he holds a sheaf of grain. Sometimes Oceanus, not Saturn, observes the birth. In some cases the two appear together, and in one case, an inscription specifically refers to the gods of the oceans and waters.

The birth scene of Mithras can probably be ranked second only to the slaying of the bull in its importance to Mithrasism. It appears frequently, has many variations and stands in relation to the bull-slaying scene much as the nativity stands in relation to the crucifixion in Christianity. The birth of Mithras marks the inauguration of hope, the beginning of the redemption of souls. By standing as a symbol of hope, it is also a promise of victory. The moment is so sacred it seems nothing will ever quite overcome it.

The Miracle of the Rock

Mithras was an archer god, and his bow and arrows appear in two acts which held clear theological import for the Mithrasians. One of these was the miracle of the rock, in which Mithras fires a single arrow into a rock or the rocky face of a mountain. From the puncture (or wound) water gushes forth. In this the rock seems to represent clouds, and the clouds in turn the "cave" that is the universe. The miracle, then, is a cosmic event. Like Mithras' own birth, it may have a significance far wider than those whom it affects, for there are witnesses to the miracle.

Variations of the scene occur. At times Cautes and Cautopates are in attendance, sometimes not. The commonest representation is of the shepherds as witnesses. Sometimes the shepherds actually beseech the god to fire the arrow. The place the arrow strikes becomes a permanent spring. In this Mithras becomes a culture hero protecting the shepherds. It may be a reference to breaking a drought, as has often been mentioned. But the spring also implies a place in some sacred geography lost to us.

The scene is not prominent in the canon art. In only one case—a relief from the Mithraeum at Dieburg—is the scene shown on its own. In all others, it appears in conjunction with other scenes.

The Great Hunt

By contrast, the great hunting scene of Mithras is particularly popular in Germanic regions of the Empire. Some representations show Mithras hunting with bow and arrow astride a horse. Some show him on horseback, but without the bow and arrows. At Dura-Europas a fairly complete version survives. It shows Mithras on a horse, at full gallop. Mithras draws his bow and unerringly hits his quarry. He is hunting some kind of stag or deer. Some of these have unusual horns which end in crescent moons. The esoteric meaning of this is unknown.

Some of the significance of the hunting scene can be gleaned by the companions with Mithras. These are the lion, the dog, and the snake. These creatures also appear in the Tauroctony scene.

Some mythological connection must exist between the two scenes. What this would be we do not know. That there was a significant meaning is further indicated by a relief at Neuenheim, in which Mithras rides at a gallop with a lion and snake by his side. In his hand he holds the globe of dominion.

It may have been the passion of some Mithrasians to hunt that accounts for the prominence of this scene. But it may also have been taken as a preparation for the task of slaying the bull, getting the god fit enough for the task. All we can say for certain is this hunting scene takes place before the Sacred Meal with Sol, and probably before the hunt for the bull.

The Slaying of the Bull

On reflection it would seem strange if an event as cosmic as the slaying of the bull should have simply happened, without preparation or aftermath. In fact there was such preparation in a titanic struggle and an aftermath in the Sacred Meal.

But the struggle, unattainable to mortals, was of great interest only in the Danubian region. Oriental and Roman Mithraea had little or no interest in these events.

The scenes shown can, roughly, be put in order. It begins with the bull grazing by itself. Mithras surprises the bull and with his great strength lifts the animal onto his own shoulders. He takes the bull to a house or sacred building. In Dieburg this is a rectangular building with a triangular roof structure. Two pillars in the form of trees are at the front of the building, forming bars to keep the bull from escaping. On the frieze of the roof are three gods which have, alas, been worn too far to be recognized.

However the bull is sometimes shown in a boat, or in a crescent moon above a boat. The Moon is on its back, as if the moon itself is a ship. In ancient art it often was so represented. In Zarathustrian scripture there is a hymn (Yast) to the soul of cattle, in which the bull that is the soul of all cattle complains it is badly treated. Where, it asks Ahura Mazda, is the one who will tend it with kindness? Mithra, is the answer.

If that Yast made it into the liturgy of the Mithrasians, the bull meets a different fate. He escapes by means unknown, careening at full speed. Mithras hangs on to the bull's neck with grim determination. Eventually the bull tires, or Mithras otherwise reasserts his power.

The next scene shows Mithras with the bull's hind legs over his shoulders, dragging it away. As Mithras hauls the bull, the bull's forelegs and muzzle drag on the ground. Mithras drags the bull into a cave, which is to say into the first Mithraeum, and holds it down. Here he slays the bull, its blood forming the trail of the Milky Way, which allowed souls to be born into our world, and to return to the starry heaven from whence they came.

Sol & Mithras

Some scholars have pointed out that Mithras slays the Bull just as the Indian Mitra slays Soma. But it has also been said Mitra acts in concert with other gods, while Mithras acts alone.

This is not true. Mithras acts in concert with, or under the orders of, Sol, Luna, and even the constellations shown in the bull-slaying scene as scorpion, lion, dog, and snake. All this assumes that the torchbearers, Cautes and Cautopates, are simply reflections of Mithras himself, whereas the evidence of art shows they predated Mithras, and even aided at his birth.

There is a central importance to Mithras' interactions with Sol which is second only to those with the bull in defining the role of the god. No other scene is so frequently—or lovingly—represented. Mithras himself was sometimes invoked as "Mithras deus Sol invictus," Mithras the invincible Sun-god. Yet he is frequently shown with the Sun-god in poses from submission to conflict to triumph to friendship. And as Ulansey was the first academic to finally observe, to choose an appropriate metaphor, grab the bull by the horns and say there must also be a "deus Sol victus," a defeated Sun-god.[1] The image of Sol fits this suggestion admirably.

I think it is a mistake to seek a single explanatory theme in the varying representations of these two gods. Vermaseren has

[1] David Ulansey, *The Origins of the Mithraic Mysteries: Cosmology and Salvation in the Ancient World* (Oxford: Oxford University Press, 1989), p. 110.

come to the same conclusion, but for different reasons, citing Professor Guthrie's contention that in the classical world, men didn't feel the need to codify their religious beliefs into a single dogmatic unity.[2] Quite true, but perhaps not in the case of Mithrasism. We are used to thinking of Christians as having a single, dogmatic body of opinions referred to a central authority. But that overlooks the massive heterogeneity which has been the reality of Christianity since its inception. We should not forget the first actually Christian act was to settle a dogmatic dispute. The chronologically oldest Christian writing we have is exactly such a dispute (the Gospels weren't written until about eighty years after this).

We should note the many disputes that arose over the nature of God were settled finally in the fourth century by the Council of Nicea. In this council Jesus was said to be fully God and fully Man, and God was said to be a trinity (the notion of which was borrowed from Platonic theory or the religion of Isis). But disputes over the relationship between the three forms of God would continue, such as the Arian theory: God the Father was greater than God the Son. Other disputes arose. For centuries after Rome fell, Christianity remained a heterodox system subject to significant dispute.

I believe theological disputes similarly vexed the Mithrasian religion, different beliefs dominating in different areas. The most serious dispute arose over two issues: the nature of adeptship and the nature of the relationship between Sol and Mithras. In both cases the Danubian and the Roman Mithraea show the differences most clearly.

In the Germanic areas, Sol was thought to have submitted most completely to Mithras. In Roman areas, an agreement is reached between the two gods. In both cases, the point at issue is the nature of the succession of power from Sol to Mithras.

That such a succession was important is shown by the representations of Jupiter and Saturn. In the classical myth, power changed hands by an overthrow—Jupiter castrated his father. In Mithrasian art the succession is by an oath—Saturn hands Jupi-

[2] M. J. Vermaseren, *Mithras, The Secret God* (London: Chatto & Windus, 1959), p. 95.

ter the thunderbolts while behind or between the two gods is an altar. This peaceful transfer heralds the change of ages from the Golden Age, sanctified by a sacrifice at the altar. This same altar of oath sometimes appears between or behind Mithras and Sol. In one case there is even meat on a skewer and a raven pecking at the meat while Sol and Mithras conclude their pact. In another example an altar appears between Sol and Mithras. Both gods carry a knife, perhaps in order to conclude a blood pact.

An altar at Poetovio may give some indication of the nature of this pact. On one face, it shows Sol and Mithras concluding their pact; on the second is inscribed a bow, a quiver of arrows, and a sword; on the third is the miracle of the rock. In this latter scene, Mithras fires the arrow to create the spring. Shepherds cup their hands to drink of the water.

The miracle of the waters is cosmic in that Mithras overcomes a drought by creating the spring. The shepherds had pleaded for relief. By obliging, Mithras sets himself on a collision course with Sol, who initiated the drought. A conflict may have ensued or Sol may simply have realized the greater power of the younger god and graciously deferred authority to him. But this resolution was not accomplished before the slaying of the bull.

In fact, in the Tauroctony Sol seems to be giving the order to Mithras to make that sacrifice. Since it was a sacrificial act from which came salvation, it changed the nature of the relationship between the divine and man.

With that change a new age was ushered in, just as in the case of Saturn and Jupiter. Perhaps this is why Saturn is sometimes shown in contemplative pose: he is thinking about the change of ages.

Sol's power is not destroyed, however; he is still the sun. But his power is now regulated by Mithras, the sun-behind-the-sun. This is shown in a scene where Sol kneels before Mithras, who places his left hand on Sol's head and holds an object in the right.

This object has been interpreted in many ways: as a drinking horn, a Phrygian cap, or a hock of meat. In fact, as Roger Beck and R. L. Gordon have pointed out, and Ulansey has supported, it could well be the leg of the Great Bear.[3]

In ancient times this constellation never set below the horizon. It was therefore associated with the axis of the universe. By this scene we are told Mithras, the stellar god, asserted his authority over the sun and guaranteed Sol would keep to his right path until the end of time. In so doing Mithras, as regulator of the universe, made salvation possible for men by giving them both time and regularity in which to discover the path.

The Sacred Meal

We don't know for certain the Sacred Meal followed the other events in the relationship between Sol and Mithras. For example, it may have been the Sacred Meal preceded the scene where Mithras holds the axis of the universe in one hand while placing a hand on the head of Sol. But we can be certain the Sacred Meal was far more important than the other events. Nothing beyond the Tauroctony itself gained such attention. Some icons of the Tauroctony are in fact set on a hinge so they can be turned around. The Sacred Meal is on the reverse side.

We can also be certain the Sacred Meal happened after the sacrifice of the bull, since in some scenes the bull's hide is shown draped over the table at which the two gods sit. In other representations Cautes and Cautopates bring the bull to the meal, the carcass slung along a pole carried over their shoulders in the way prizes of the hunt have been carried since time immemorial.

Sometimes Mithras is seated on the right, sometimes on the left. The murals thus do not show any consistency of who sits in the dominant (right) position, so it is not clear whether the meal precedes or follows the change of dominance from Sol to Mithras.

Mithrasians normally represent Sol as naked save for a riding whip, a radiant halo, and a short red cloak. Only at the Sacred

[3] Cited in Ulansey, *The Origins of the Mithraic Mysteries*, pp. 105-106.

Meal is he clothed. The Aventine Mithraeum shows him clad in a long red robe with a yellow belt.

We know the Mithrasians imitated this meal, with the Pater and the Heliodromus imitating the gods. The Pater was commonly dressed in a manner similar to that of Mithras, the Heliodromus had a uniform of a red robe with a yellow belt.

At this Sacred Meal, Sol gives Mithras a bunch of grapes. He is offering Mithras the secret of wine. It was Sol's contribution to the earth-born god who became a god of the stars.

The wine operated as a substitute for the blood of the bull. It and the bread and meat of the Sacred Meal fulfilled the promise of the god of human salvation. Though Mithras was no longer among his followers his promise remained.

The Ascension

With his ascension to the heavens, Mithras fulfilled his promise to his followers. Mithras was no longer on Earth. Having given his message of hope to the world, Mithras leaves it to take up his position as cosmic ruler (kosmokrater). He does this by getting into Sol's horse-drawn chariot and heading to the sky, or to the oceans of space. Sometimes Sol is in the chariot with him. Sometimes Mithras actually runs along beside or behind the chariot. But the message of his ascension is always clear.

Danubian Mithraea show Mithras heading toward Ocean the god or wavy lines. Roman Mithraea show him heading toward the sky. The theological distinction this signified we do not yet understand. Possibly it indicated a distinction between a Mithras whom Danubian followers conceptualized as more remote or abstract, while Roman followers saw him in the familiar course of the sun. Perhaps the Danubians saw Mithras more in the light of Mithra and his invincible chariot drawn by four horses.

It is to our poverty that the liturgy has been destroyed. It was destroyed by rivals bent on domination, who saw anything but submission to them as a threat. The Mithrasians sought to support, to reform, and to purify the world they knew. When that world was washed away in a tide of barbarian invasion, the Mithrasians were seemingly destroyed with it.

But by the preservation of the Mithraea, by the art, and most of all by those constellations which still walk the path of the Milky Way, the god of Roman mysteries lives up to his title "invictus." Lodged securely in the heavens, the god is invincible, and defies the hands of mortal men to tear him down.

BIBLIOGRAPHY

Actes de Congrès. *Etudes Mithriaques*. Tehran: Bibliothèque Pahlavi, distributed by E. J. Brill, Leiden, 1978.
Despite the title, much of it is in English. This is the record
of the second congress on Mithraic studies (see Hinnells for
the first congress). Possibly not for the faint-hearted, as chapter titles like "Bagda and Mithra in Sogdiana" and "Mithra's
Planetary Setting in the Coinage of the Great Kushans'" show.

Arnott, Peter. *Introduction to the Roman World*. London: Sphere
Books, 1970.
Chapter 9 deals with the religious nature of the Empire.

Barber, Richard. *The Knight and Chivalry*. London: Cardinal,
1970.
The references to the Knights Templar are useful, and the
book as a whole puts them into the perspective of their times.
As such it is useful in comparing the Templars to the Mithrasians.

Boyce, Mary. *Zoroastrians: Their Religious Beliefs and Practices*.
London: Routledge & Kegan Paul, 1979.
Boyce's sympathy with the religion and her ability to see to its
heart are invaluable. Her respect for Zarathustra's vision as
he meant it, not as Western academics would like to see it, is
invaluable, for studying not only that religion, but Mithra as
well.

Burkert, Walter. *Ancient Mystery Cults*. Cambridge: Harvard University Press, 1987.
Good information, but given to the belief that the world we
have was somehow inevitable.

Chuvin, Pierre. *A Chronicle of the Last Pagans.* Trans. by B. A. Archer. Cambridge: Harvard University Press, 1990.
Deals with Mithrasism only tangentially, but it does give some view of the society and times.

Colquhoun, Ithell. *Sword of Wisdom: MacGregor Mathers and the Golden Dawn.* New York: G. P. Putnam's Sons, 1975.
Describes the ideas and personalities of the Golden Dawn, providing a good basis for my comparison of the Golden Dawn and the Mithrasian religion in chapter 2.

Cumont, Franz. *The Mysteries of Mithra.* 2nd rev. ed. Trans. from French by Thomas J. McCormack. New York: Dover Publications, 1903.
This is the work that really commenced the whole study. It must be read, if only to discover what everyone else is disagreeing with.

Dewar, James. *The Unlocked Secret: Freemasonry Examined.* London: Corgi Books, 1966.
A thorough look at the organization and mystique of the Freemasons, suitable for comparison with the Mithrasian religion.

Dietrerich, Erlautert Von Albert. *Eine Mithrasliturgie.* Darmstadt: Wissenschaftliche Buchgesellschaft, 1966.
Its claim to be a liturgy of Mithras remains controversial, but those who can read German may wish to decide for themselves.

Gershevitch, Ilya, trans. *The Avestan Hymn to Mithra.* London: Cambridge University Press, 1959.
Excellent translation of the Yast, with commentary and a highly useful introduction. Has weathered more recent scholarship quite well.

Godwin, Joscelyn. *Mystery Religions in the Ancient World.* London: Thames & Hudson, 1981.

I disagree with much that Godwin says, and suggest a misunderstanding of the nature of Mithras, Serapis, and even early Christianity. That said, it is a fine work in which there is a great deal of value from an author generally sympathetic to the mysteries.

Henig, Martin. *Religion in Roman Britain*. London: B. T. Batsford, Ltd., 1984.
The chapter on Mithrasian and other eastern religions is quite useful. Includes the floor plan of the London Mithraeum.

Hinnell, John R., ed. *Mithraic Studies: Proceedings of the First International Congress of Mithraic Studies*. Manchester: Manchester University Press, 1975, 2 vols.
This work is a lot more readable than the title suggests, although some of the speeches are not in English. Articles like "The Role of the Roman Army in the Spread and Practice of Mithraism," "Some Thoughts on Isis in Relation to Mithras," and "Mithras and Christ: Some Iconographical Similarities," show the diversity of the two volumes.

Howarth, Stephen. *The Knights Templar.* London: Collins, 1982.
A good history of the Order and its beliefs, suitable for extending the comparisons I made in chapter 2 between the Mithrasian religion and the Knights Templar.

Howe, Ellic. *The Magicians of the Golden Dawn: A Documentary History of a Magical Order 1887-1923*. York Beach, ME: Samuel Weiser, 1972.
Chapter 2 compares the Mithrasian religion with the Golden Dawn. This history covers the organization of the latter group.

Jones, Bernard E. *Freemasons' Guide and Compendium*. London: Harrap, Ltd., 1950, rev. ed. 1956.
Useful for my comparison between Masonic tracing boards and the Tauroctonies of the Mithrasian religion.

168 — D. Jason Cooper

Knight, Stephen. *The Brotherhood: The Secret World of the Free-masons.* London: Granada, 1984.
This book caused quite a sensation when it came out, though it said little new. It does serve to show the attitudes which can be drummed against a group with secrets, and to show how a society with secrets often must recruit by friendship link rather than theology.

Malandra, William W., ed. & trans. *An Introduction to Ancient Iranian Religion: Readings from the Avesta and Achaemenid Inscriptions.* Minneapolis: University of Minnesota Press, 1983.
Includes the Yast to Mithra as well as other material. Good introduction.

Merkelbach, Reinhold. *Mithras.* Konigstein: Verlag Anton Hain Meisenheim, 1984.
The fact that it is in German will be an impediment for most readers, which is a pity. But almost everybody can understand and appreciate the copious plates at the back and the different charts and illustrations throughout the book.

Olmstead, A. T. *History of the Persian Empire.* Chicago: University of Chicago Press, 1948.
See the index references to Mitanni, Mitra, Aryan religions and Aryan tribes.

Partner, Peter. *The Murdered Magicians: The Templars and their Myth.* Oxford: Oxford University Press, 1982.
Deals with the reputation of the Templars after Le Bell's heinous acts. But the kind of comparisons made to Freemasonry can also enhance the comparisons I made between the Templars and the Mithrasians in chapter 2 of this work.

Porphyry. *On the Cave of the Nymphs.* Translation and introductory essay by Robert Lamberton. Barrytown, NY: Station Hill Press, 1983.

Not actually a book on Mithras, but the first book of literary criticism in the Western World. It contains a number of asides about Mithras which historians have been using to unravel the religion.

Richmond, I. A. *Roman Britain*. London: Penguin Books, 1955, 2nd ed., 1963.
Only the chapter on religion has anything to do with the Mithrasian religion, and here I think he's got the nature of the thing wrong.

Short, Martin. *Inside the Brotherhood: Further Secrets of the Freemasons.* London: Grafton Books, 1989.
A large and rather unsympathetic treatment of the Masonic organization. But it does provide a good basis for comparing the Masons with the Mithrasian religion, and how others might have reacted to a group whose existence was known but whose internal workings were not.

Speidel, Michael P. *Mithras-Orion: Greek Hero and Roman Army God.* Leiden: E.J. Brill, 1980.
Ulansey says Mithras is the constellation Perseus; Speidel says he is Orion. Even though both have something of value to contribute, neither is an occultist and this has blinkered them somewhat.

Ulansey, David. *The Origins of the Mithraic Mysteries: Cosmology and Salvation in the Ancient World.* Oxford: Oxford University Press, 1990.
One of a new breed of theorists who see the bull-slaying scene as an astronomical, not eschatological, device.

Vermaseren, M. J. *Corpus Inscriptionum et monumentorum religionis mithriacae.* 2 volumes. The Hague: Martinus Nijhoff, 1956.
Replaces an older work by Cumont. It is essentially a collection of the archaeological material.

Mithras, The Secret God. London: Chatto & Windus, 1959. A very good book but now somewhat out of date. It was written when Cumont still dominated the topic.

Mithraica I: The Mithraeum at S. Maria Capua Verte. Leiden: E. J. Brill, 1971.

Mithraica II: The Mithraeum at Ponza. Leiden: E. J. Brill, 1974.

Mithraica III: The Mithraeum at Marino. Leiden: E. J. Brill, 1982.

Mithraica IV: Le Monument D'Ottaviano Zéno et le Culte de Mithra Sur le Celius. Leiden: E. J. Brill, 1978.
Each of these works details one individual Mithraeum. Because of extensive use of pictures, even the last (the only one not in English) is of considerable value.

Walsh, Michael. *The Triumph of the Meek: Why Early Christianity Succeeded.* San Francisco: HarperCollins, 1986.
An interesting but limited examination of Christianity, but takes the religion as both predestined to win and somehow operating in a kind of vacuum.

Index

G

Gemini, 71
gems, 51
Gershevitch, Ilya, 1, 6, 7
Gnostics, 15
god of light, 22, 44
Golden Age, 161
Golden Dawn, 26, 27, 29, 42,
44, 45, 70, 118, 122, 130,
137, 145, 146
Graves, Robert, 51
great hunt, 157
Grimes, Prof. D. W., 92

H

Hanged Man, 64
harpe, 133
Hecate, 49, 58
Heliodromus, 27, 28, 51, 55,
57, 113, 131, 134, 138,
142, 153
helmet, 116
Hinnells, John R., 125
Hittites, 1, 143
Holy Immortals, 7
homosexual element, 115
honey, 125, 132
Howe, Ellic, 70
Hydra, 66, 67, 69, 71, 74, 125,
127

I

icon, 68
initiation, 19, 45, 54, 86-88,
116, 123, 144
ritual, 152
ipsissimu, 137
Iranian Pantheon, 1
Isis, 16, 22, 51, 126

J

Jupiter, 34, 50, 56, 125, 126,
129, 160, 161
Justin, 142

K

King Antiochus, 8, 77
Knights Templar, 31, 118, 136
korb, 58
kosmokrater, 163

L

lamp, 122
lance, 116
le Belle, Phillipe, 32
Leo, 24, 26-28, 33, 46, 54-56,
67-69, 71, 74, 75, 113, 116,
124, 125, 127, 129, 130,
131, 142, 150
Liberator, 144